Billiard Atlas

ON

Systems & Techniques

Volume 3

Walter Harris

"The Billiard Atlas"
P.O. Box 321426
Cocoa Beach, Florida 32932-1426

http://www.billiardsatlas.com
e-mail: wharris@billiardsatlas.com

Copyright 1996 by Walt Harris

Printed in the United States

All rights reserved. No part of this publication may be copied, stored in a retrieval system, or transmitted, in any form or any means, recording, electronic photocopying, mechanical or otherwise, without the prior written permission of the author.

This sets forth U. S. copyright relations with other independent nations of the world. Argentina, Austria, Belgium, Bolivia, Brazil, Czechoslovakia, Chile, China, Columbia, Costa Rica, Croatia, Denmark, Ecuador, El Salvador, France, Germany, Greece, Guatemala, Holland, Honduras, Hungary, Italy, Japan, Nicaragua, Peru, Portugal, Philippines, Poland, Spain, Soviet Union, Thailand, Turkey, Venezuela, Vietnam, and Yugoslavia.

Published May 1996.
Reprinted October 2000.

Preface

An arsenal of new weapons for the three cushion billiard player

The nine ball player can now learn more about the game

Table of Contents

Preface	Introduction	C I to XII
Chapter One	The Long Angle	C-1
Chapter Two	Across the Table	C-31
Chapter Three	Some Gems	C-59
Chapter Four	End Rail	C-71
Chapter Five	How To	C-97
Chapter Six	The Short Game	C-117
Chapter Seven	Fundamentals	C-135
Chapter Eight	The Mental Side	C-149
Chapter Nine	Equipment	C-157
Chapter Ten	Miscellaneous	C-169
Credits, Index		C-187

Searching for valuable material seemed endless, thanks to dearest *Johanna* for her enthusiasm and encouragement.

My thanks to *Joe Ventrelli* for his many hours on the billiard table making sure these systems and techniques were accurate.

Introduction

A tremendous evolution of the game has taken place in Europe and parts of Asia. No one is any longer surprised if a player reaches a game average of 2.00; only averages of 3.00 are remarkable.

Players from the Western Hemisphere, and probably in most other parts of the globe, are still playing the same averages of forty years ago, which are between .700 and .900. A 1.00 average is rare. One of the main reasons is a lack of knowledge of the diamond systems. This is the calculation of the shots with help from the diamond marks on the rails. A lot of players have much ambition in other phases of the game, but are not interested in the marks on the rails.

Enrique Navarra won the world title in 1954 and 1958, with averages of .937 and .926. In 1970, **Raymond Ceulemans** won it with a 1.267 average, so you can see that the stratospheric averages of today are of recent vintage.

In my travels, I've found that most billiard players don't know how to improve their game. Most play by feel, and rarely is anyone around to help them. The experienced room players were unable to supply the answers. They too, were basically mired at their level of play, mostly playing by the seat of their pants.

It is impossible to be a top player without the knowledge of systems and techniques, unless a player has an IQ of 160 and plays billiards six hours a day for years. Another possibility is, that a player could have devoted many years to the balk-line game, have much talent, and have taken years of lessons from great teachers.

A talented person devoting his life work to billiards may be able to reach a 1.0 level of play, but for the rest of the billiard world, using "feel" only may just get them to be a decent room player.

If you want to verify this, just ask good experienced players what they know about the "plus shot", or how accurate they are on bank shots, or how they adjust to corner-hit angles. A player needs information to calculate these shots otherwise he is lost.

Many players, who do not use systems subconsciously, think a master system may exist that solves all problems. This is not so. There is no master "diamond system" that calculates all the running lines. For example, how could there be a master plan when a dead ball shot is attempted, or a double the rail, or a reverse the rail, or a spin shot, or very short angles, etc.

The goal of these "Atlas" books is to provide the player with the required know-how to handle any shot. Learning how to calculate running lines can begin quickly; memorizing the many running lines will probably take a while.

When a student embraces only one system or technique, he will know more about that shot when it arises, and his entire game will be better. Instead of a 5.6 player, he may be a 5.7 player. Getting to be a better player is fun, but it takes time and study.

These "Billiard Atlas" books contain a variety of ball systems that differ from each other. Most non-system players do not realize that this kind of information exists. In fact, many players do not hit dead ball shots. When these systems are absorbed, the player will have a "set" to choose from, which will provide a great edge in determining how to play a shot. This will shave off many years in becoming a better player.

The great *Raymond Cuelemans* is mainly responsible for our present level of billiard play, and a major champion of system use. Top-level play requires knowing the running lines and being able to execute the shot.

Foreword

Writing about billiard systems and techniques is not easy. As a reporter, I have to understand the technical components that are being written about, and then write the manual for an audience who may not understand the English language.

My task is to communicate complex concepts as effectively and as simply as possible, and many times this is difficult. For example, when the subject of stroke is discussed, my descriptions do not do justice to this subject, since many chapters could be written here. The "*Billiard Atlas 3*" only covers some highlights.

Volume 3 had me searching the globe for books and periodicals, mostly in other languages. This, in turn, involved the problem of finding a billiard player that would offer his services as a translator.

Global systems players volunteered their services by submitting material for these "Atlas" books. Thanks to them, and the translators, we have new data to use.

In addition to the above, information from the top players was an important part. Many thanks for their generosity.

Passing important information onto the billiard world is definitely a labor of love, and for me, it is a great privilege to write on the subject of billiards.

Chapter One

The Long Angle

This chapter will take you on an unusual instruction trip. In my forty-five years of playing billiards, this kind of long angle information has not been available.

Very few players know the exact running lines of long angle patterns.

This chapter will introduce four new systems. The *"Two Thirds," "Florida Back Up," "Sid's Cousin"* and how to *"Triangulate."* You will soon be attempting types of billiard patterns you never dreamed had calculations.

"System South" helps to become more accurate when this billiard pattern presents itself. During the past years, using "feel only" for this did not increase billiard production.

When alternatives are dim, The *"Lucky Five"* system will give you a chance to score certain low percentage shots.

When you embrace the information in this chapter, your game will look different, and you will be scoring billiards the average player does not attempt.

System South

This system belongs to an entire family of shots, and as of this writing, information making this shot easier, was not available. A good player once started to describe this method but did not elaborate, as he had second thoughts about passing on his good information.

Word has it that this method originated from Peru, its author unknown, but thanks to **Stephen Cook,** we now have it.

Drawing 1 has the cue ball origin from the third diamond, and this will be called the zero line. Employ cue ball english as indicated.

Drawing 2 has the same cue ball origin, but with three new object-ball locations. The numbers on the short rail indicate the cue-ball english that should be employed.

Drawing 3 now moves the cue-ball origin. The zero line uses cue ball english as shown in drawing 1. The long rail numbers indicate cue-ball english needed when the cue ball is away from the zero line.

Drawing 4 shows an example where a variation takes place and the cue ball is going from end rail to end rail. My best guess is to use minus one cue tip of english, maybe a minus ½ tip.

Drawing 1

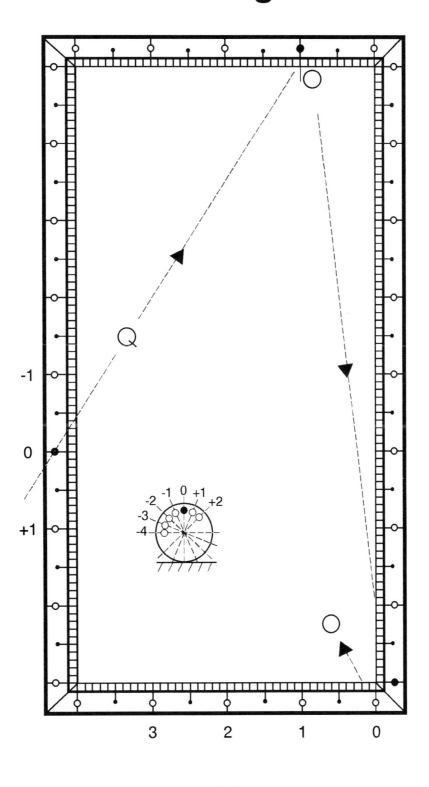

C-3

Drawing 2

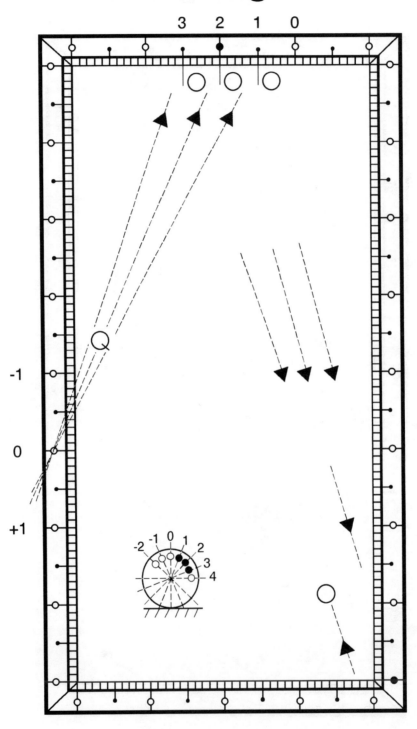

C-4

Drawing 3

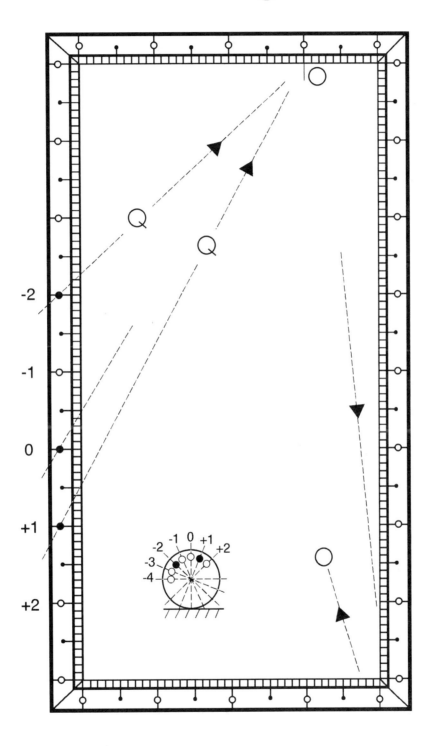

C-5

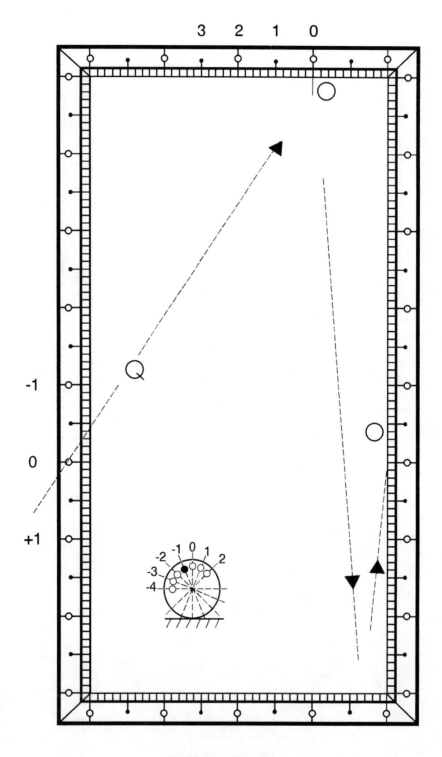

Drawing 4

C-6

For long angle shots with running english, strike the cue ball with a moderate-to-soft speed.

■

With this speed, the cue ball curve and deflection basically cancel each other out.

Two-Thirds System

Sometimes a player needs to know a path that is outside of "normal running-english" paths, and this dead-ball system helps.

Drawing 5 indicates the cue ball origin numbers on the long rail. Note these numbers turn the corner onto the short rail.

The return paths are about 66% of the cue-ball origin number.

These numbers are to be slightly altered when testing the table, especially on new rail cloth.

Drawing 5 shows an example where the cue-ball origin is at diamond 8, and the return is 66% of diamond 8, or 5.3.

Drawing 6 indicates how this system is applied to a normal billiard situation.

Notice that this system stops at a cue ball origin of 12. If you wish to use numbers on the short rail that are larger than 12, use the "*New York Bob System,*" *as shown in The Billiard Atlas II.*

These guidelines make scoring billiards easier and add to a player's arsenal of knowledge.

Drawing 5

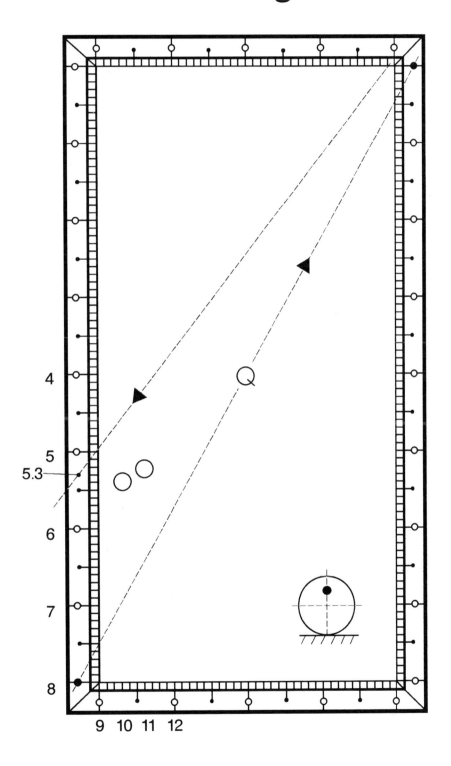

Drawing 6

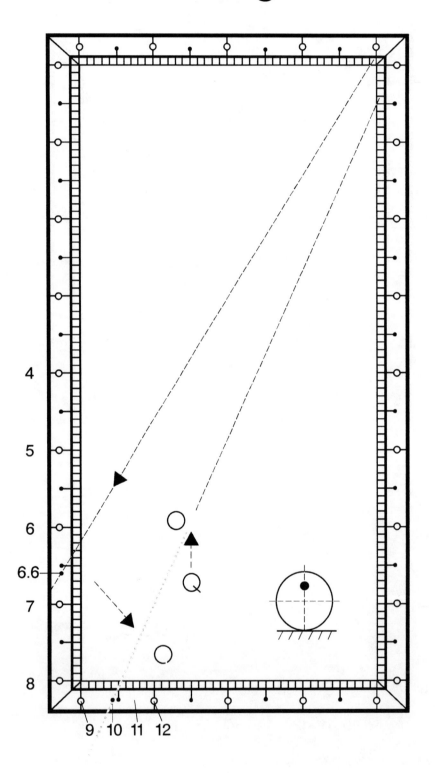

C-10

The two most important items in scoring a billiard are, perfect speed and hitting the cue ball exactly as you planned.

Lucky Five

Knowing this method will get you out of some difficult situations. It's just an easy dead-ball system called Lucky Five. Note that the cue-ball origin is from the end rail.

When the cue ball is aimed at zero, on the adjacent long rail, *add five* to the third-rail cue-ball origin point to determine the third rail hit point. Drawings 7, 8 and 9 reveal cue ball origins of 5, 10 and 15. When the cue ball is aimed at zero, it returns to the third rail at 10, 15 and 20.

When the cue-ball origin point is at 10, and you wish to hit 19 on the third rail, then allowances are needed. The diamond numbers on the adjacent long rail enter into the calculations. Drawing 10 has the cue-ball origin at 5, which has an allowance factor of *2 times*.

If you want to hit 12 instead of 10, the *2 times* allowance is used. It works like this: the cue ball, when aimed at zero, would return to 10 on the third rail, and if you want 12, which is 2 more than the 10, just multiply *2 times 1* and add this to 10. The new long rail aim point is 1, or diamond one. If you want 14 on the third rail, which is 4 more than the 10, multiply *2 times 2*, and then add this to 10. The new aim point on the long rail is diamond two.

Drawing 11 has the cue-ball origin at 10 and has an allowance factor of *4 times*. If you wish to hit 19 on the third rail, or four more than the normal return of 15, multiply *4 times 1*. When added to 15, this makes 19. Aim at diamond number 1 on the long rail.

Drawing 12 has the cue-ball origin at two, and this has *no* allowance factor. When aimed at zero, returns to 7 (add 5). If you want to arrive at 9, aim at diamond 2 on the long rail, and 2 plus 7 equals 9.

Note: Use the same angle from second to third rail for the angle of the third rail, to fourth rail destination.

Drawing 7

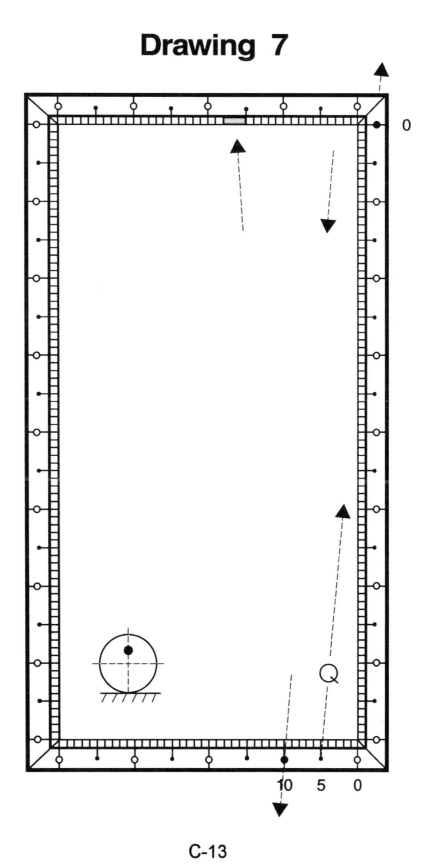

Drawing 8

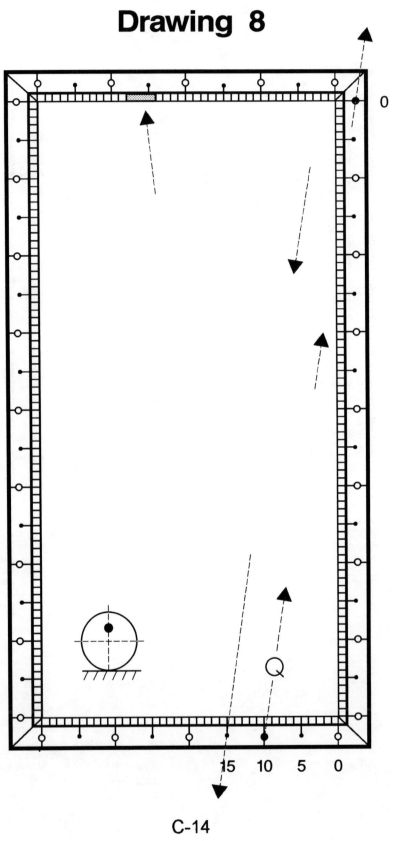

C-14

Drawing 9

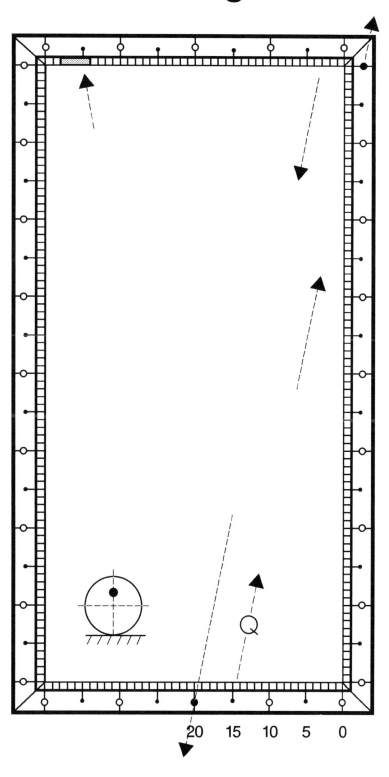

C-15

Drawing 10

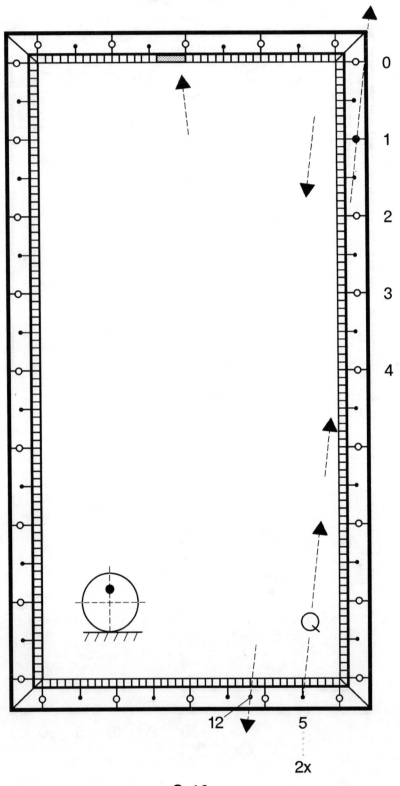

Drawing 11

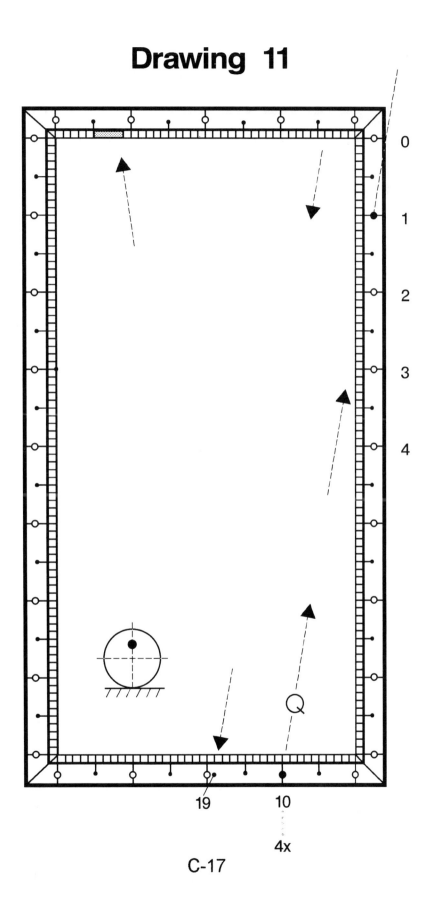

C-17

Drawing 12

C-18

The mere having of definite objective points will wonderfully improve your execution

Florida Back-up

Try this shot on your favorite opponent and you are liable to get a cue tapping for being so imaginative. These paths come in handy when the cue ball caroms off an object ball and the cue-ball paths are known.

Drawing 13 demonstrates the type of billiard attempted and maps out the numbers for the rails. Note the unusual numbers on rail "P." These cue ball origin numbers, when matched with the same numbers on the first rail, will hit corner "X."

Drawing 14 introduces a fourth-rail hit spot and the allowance numbers (circled numbers) required to score this billiard. The cue ball is going from the short-rail origin, to a long rail, to the short rail (third rail,) and then to the fourth rail hit point.

The cue-ball origin is 10 and has a circled number of 4. If you want to arrive at diamond 2 on the fourth rail, multiply 4 (circled number), by the fourth-rail hit point (2), or 4 x 2 = 8. This number now alters the basic path of 10 (cue-ball origin) to 10 (first-rail hit point) by 8, so the new first-rail hit spot is now 2.

Drawing 15 has the fourth-rail hit spot at 4, with a cue-ball origin at 20, and a circled number of 3. A rail P origin of 20, to 20 on rail N, arrives at corner X. But we wish to arrive at the fourth diamond on the final fourth rail, so multiply 3 (circled number) by 4 (fourth rail) = 12. This alters the 20 (rail P) to 20 (first-rail) line, by 12, (20 minus 12 = 8. The new first rail hit spot is 8.

Drawing 16 has the fourth-rail hit spot at 8, and a cue-ball origin of 40, which has a circled number of 1.0. A cue-ball origin of 40 (see rail P) aimed at 40 on rail N gets the cue ball to corner X. But I wish to reach diamond 8 on the fourth rail, so multiply 8 (fourth rail) by 1.0 (circled) = 8. Alter the 40-to-40 line by 8, which means aim at 32.

Drawing 13

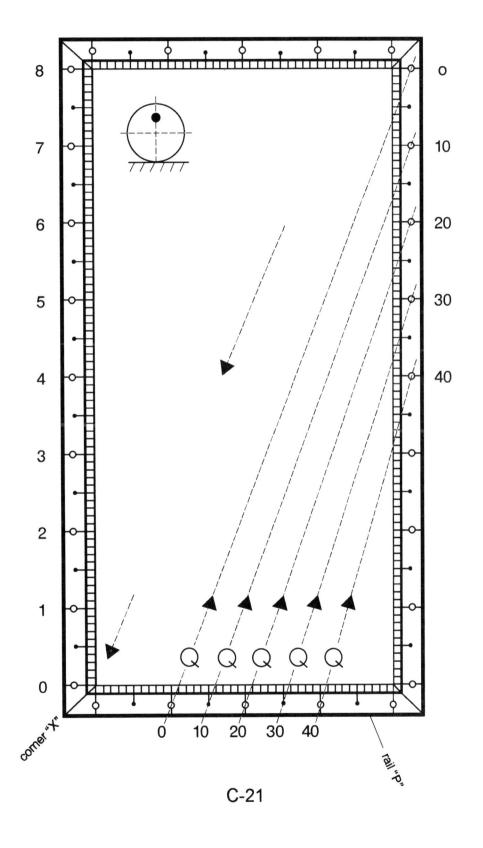

C-21

Drawing 14

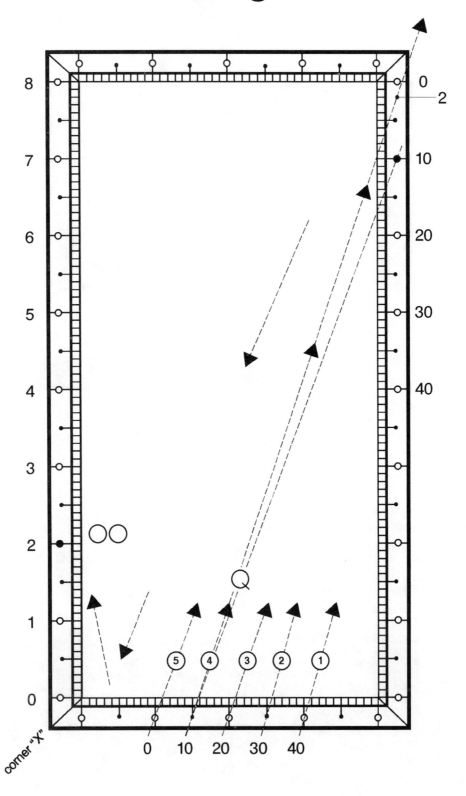

C-22

Drawing 15

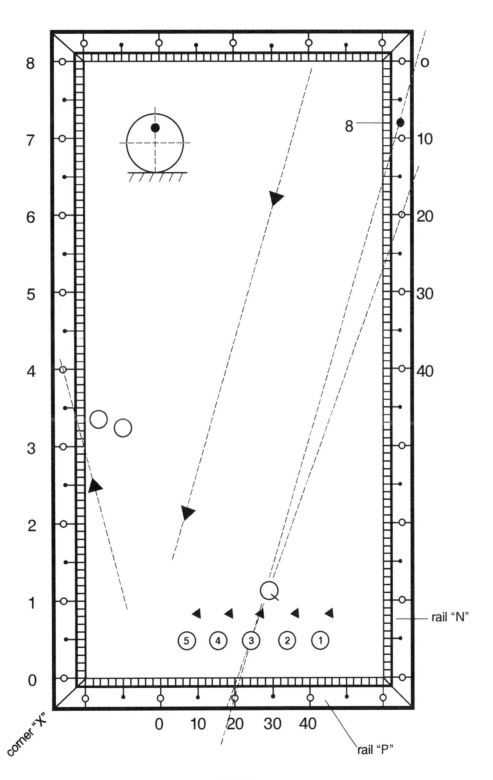

C-23

Drawing 16

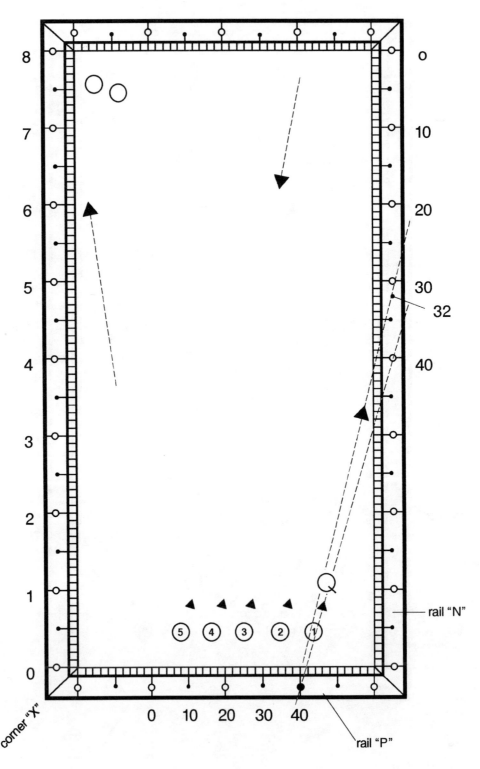

C-24

***Use just enough bridge
length to drive the
cue ball to its destination***

■

***The longer the bridge,
the more chance for error***

■

Use a firm bridge

Sid's Cousin

If the cue-ball origin was from the lower short rail, then the "Sid" system, as shown in the Billiard Atlas 1, could be the best shot selection.

Drawing 17 shows a shot with great flair, but who knows the angle? Learn to triangulate, and save the moment. This system is a bit complicated, but so is billiards.

By viewing the shot, the second-rail hit spot is estimated at Point X. Draw a line from Point X to the first-rail edge Point B.

Another line is drawn from the center of the cue ball to the first-rail edge Point A.

Another line is now drawn between Point X and Point A.

Then a line is drawn from Point B through the center of the cue ball. Find where these lines intersect, and you have almost solved the problem.

All that remains is to draw a line from this intersecting point to the first-rail Point Y. Aim at the diamond marking at Point Y, not the rail edge.

The cue ball is hit softly with dead-ball english. Use a level cue and a full follow-through stroke.

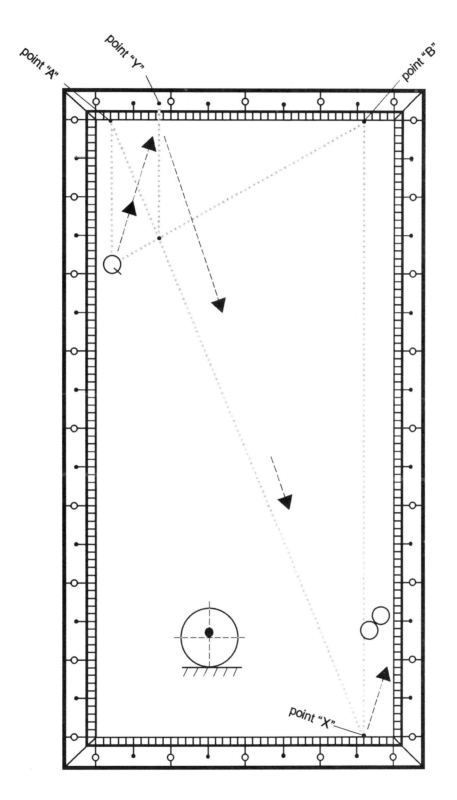

Drawing 17

C-27

Bank Tickie

The shot selections appear bleak in drawing 18, with the cue ball and one object ball frozen to a rail. A bank tickie seems to be the best prospect for success if you know the running lines.

Triangulation is selected to map out the cue-ball paths.

By estimating the cue-ball path and using dead-ball english, Point X is selected as the second-rail hit point.

A line is drawn from Point X to the first rail struck, or Point B. Another line is drawn from the cue ball center to the same first rail Point A.

Connect a line between Point A and Point X then connect another line between the cue ball (rail-contact point) and Point B.

Mark a point on the table where these two lines intersect. From this point draw a line to the first-rail Point Y. Point Y is on the diamond, not the rail edge.

Point Y is the new aim point using dead-ball english. Employ a level cue, four-rail cue-ball speed, and a full follow-through stroke.

Once you decide on using this method, the time required to map it out should be less then fifteen seconds....or less then ten seconds, with sufficient practice.

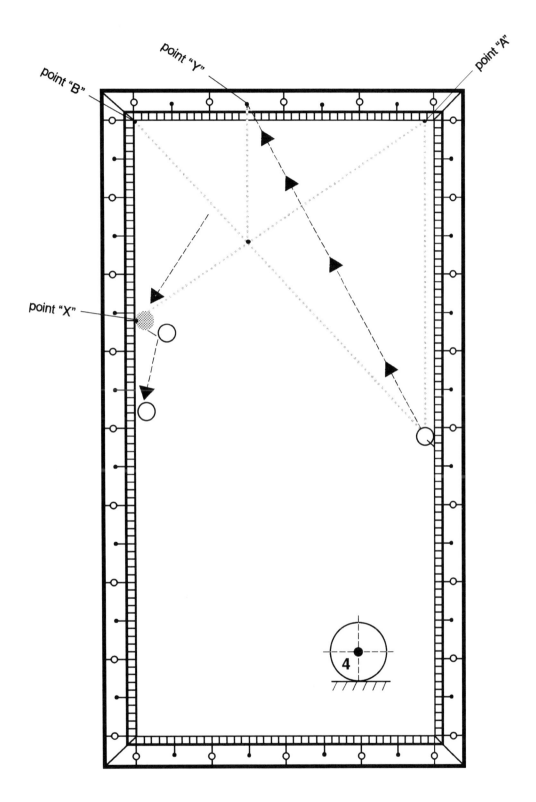

Drawing 18
C-29

Chapter Two

Across The Table

Probably the shot that separates the best from the rest is the across-the-table shot. The top players are consistently accurate.

This chapter will provide enough information so you too can execute these shots with aplomb.

The *Basic Across* method will pinpoint the running lines, and it will include the twice across-the-table patterns.

The *Dive Back* is my favorite, since you hardly ever see this shot missed by the best, and it's very forgiving.

The *Spread 2.8,* and the *Spread 1.4,* is mandatory in any players' arsenal. There are simply too many occasions where this shot can be used.

The *Max Across, Triangulation*, and *Equal Angle* systems are important, and should be part of a players' repertoire.

Easy Across

This first rate system deals with an across the table shot that goes from a long rail, to a long rail, to a short rail. Please note that we employ the use of another system.

The second rail aim point is often the missing link for establishing the complete path to the billiard, better yet, you are shown where the *side* of the cue ball hits the nose of the third rail.

Estimate where the cue ball hits the nose of the first cushion (rail M). Next, imagine the cue ball frozen to rail M at that point. Place your cue stick through the middle of the imaginary cue ball and find the cue ball origin diamond number (rail M). Now employ the *Sid System** to find the second rail hit point.

Have the cue ball arrive at the second rail with as little side english as possible. The cue ball is hit one-half tip low and a minimum of side english with medium speed, and elevate cue butt slightly.

Drawing 19 selected the third rail hit point (rail edge) at 2.0. The cue ball origin is at diamond "D", which is four half diamonds away from point "X". Each half diamond has a value of 2.0. Multiply 4 by 2.0 = 8, which is the second rail aim point.

Drawing 20 selected the third rail edge hit point at 3.0. The cue ball origin from point D, is four half diamonds from point "X". Multiply 4 times 3.0 = 12 and this is the 2nd rail aim point.

Drawing 21 has the cue ball going twice across the table. Use a third rail hit point of 5.5. Point D is the cue ball origin and is four half diamonds away from point "X". Each half diamond has a value of 5.5, thus, 4 times 5.5 = 22. Now aim for 22 on the second rail.

*See chapter one, of the "Billiard Atlas I"

Drawing 19

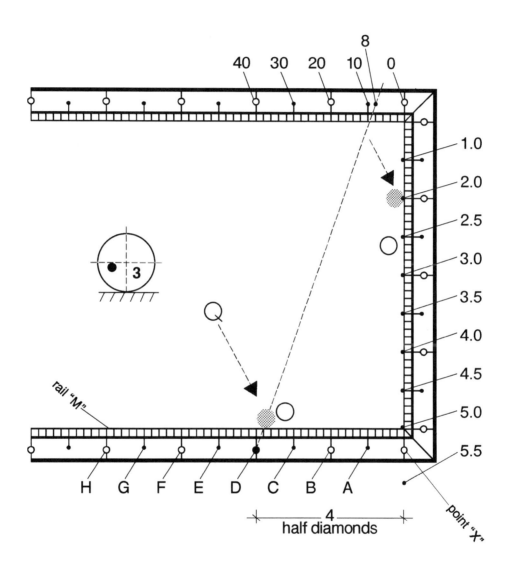

Drawing 20

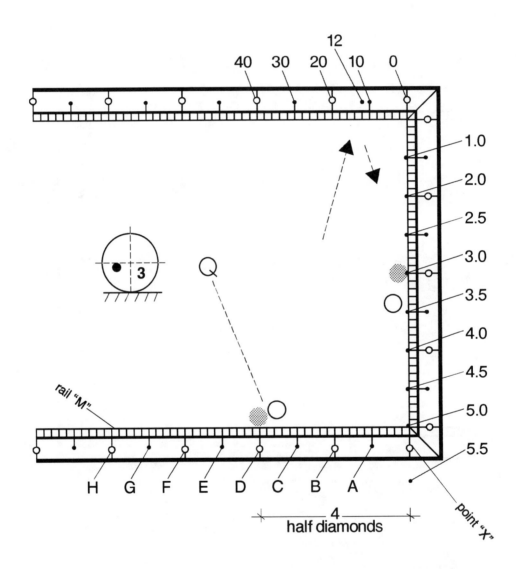

Drawing 21

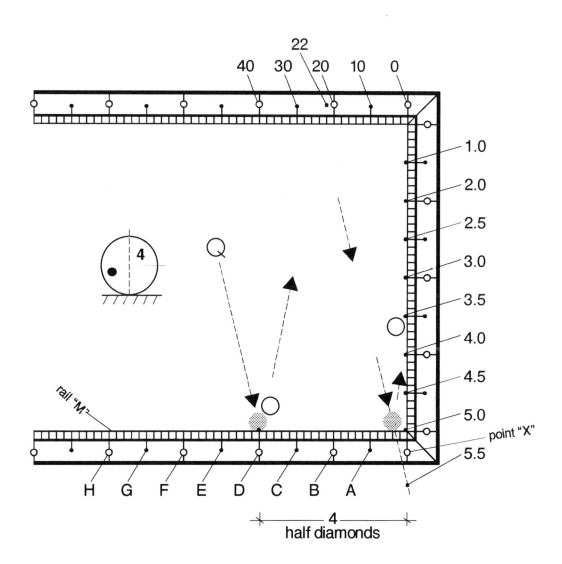

C-35

Dive Back

This technique will warm the cockles of a player's heart. It's one that satisfies, because it looks much harder than it is. It also *makes twice-across-the-table* shots, much easier.

This technique was obtained during a lesson from **Richard Bitalis**.

Drawing 22 indicates that a *twice-across-the-table shot* was selected. This shot is all "feel" and the main technique in this shot is to drive the cue ball into the first object ball, go *backwards* to the second rail, then *dive forward* into the third rail.

The cue ball english is high center, with side cue ball english that varies. Hit this with authority, lots of authority, because instead of a three-rail carom, this can be a five-rail carom.

More billiards is scored from this technique than you can imagine.

Drawing 22

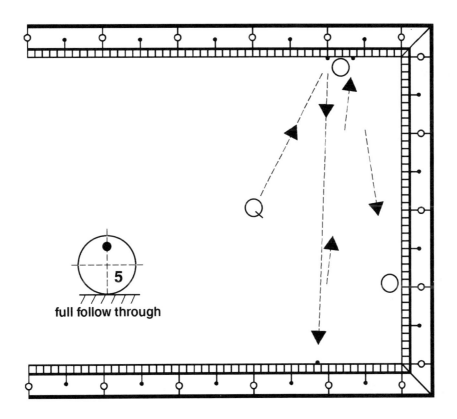

Spread 2.8

Drawing 23 has the cue-ball origin at Point A, and the first-rail aim point is B. Using a certain stroke and 4:30 cue-ball english, the cue ball should return to Point "A."

This stroke is similar to a pool stroke when you want to stop the cue ball at the point of object-ball impact. It's not a draw shot, although low english is used. This has a spread of about 2.8 diamonds, 1.4 diamonds forward and 1.4 diamonds back. If you use a full follow-through stroke, the spread will be greater then 2.8.

This technique has a cue ball "float" to the target, with the cue ball reaching the second rail with little side english. This still maintains the desired angle. Once the player has the feel for this shot, it is easy to remember.

Drawing 24 displays an across-the-table shot. The cue ball is caromed off the first object ball, sometimes backwards, then forward towards Point X on the second rail. If the player uses a long follow-through stroke, the cue ball will have too much reverse english when it hits Point "X" and this amount of cue ball english can ruin this billiard.

It is desirable to have the cue ball hit the Point "X" with little side english, so that the last object ball becomes a larger target.

To accomplish this, employ a quick forward-reverse stroke, and raise the cue butt a bit. The angle from the first object ball to the short rail is the variable. This method will restrain side english from having its full effect, and the cue ball will appear to "float in."

For the player to become familiar with the stroke and angle of return, drawing 24 illustrates the exact exercise to practice.

Drawing 23

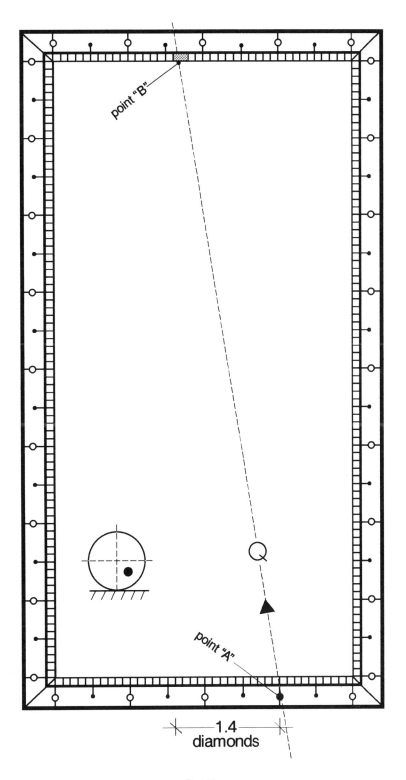

C-39

Drawing 24

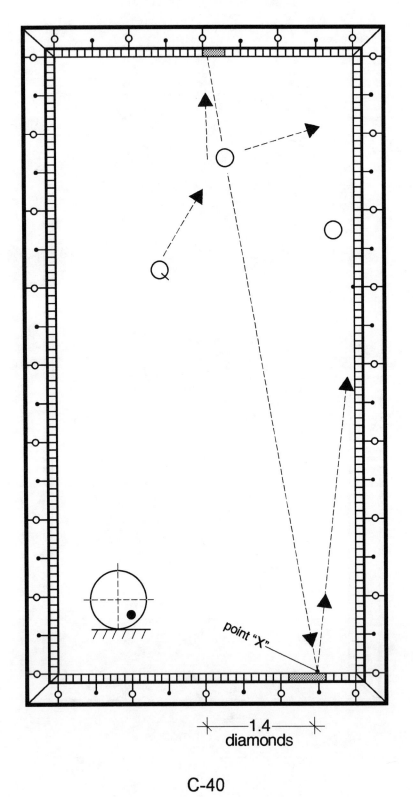

1.4 diamonds

point "X"

C-40

When rolling the cue ball for the break shot, try a five inch follow-through stroke and use a center ball hit, with a half tip of high english

Spread 1.4

Most room players will not attempt this shot because they don't understand how it's done. This is a variation of a shot that is shown elsewhere in this book, except it's on the "small table" instead of the full size table.

Previously, it was determined that the spread, when going from short rail to short rail, was 2.8 diamonds (see page 38.) When using the "small" table, and going from long rail to long rail, it's 1.4 diamonds.

A quick-forward-reverse stroke is employed, because minimum cue ball english is needed off the second-rail hit point. The angle will do the work.

Drawing 25 has the cue ball going from Point X, to Point Y, and back to Point X.

The total spread is 1.4 diamonds. The cue ball path is 0.7 of a diamond forward and 0.7 of a diamond back.

Drawing 26 has the cue ball caroming off the first object ball "backwards" to Point A. The dashed line shows an estimated backward-angle path. This angle, from Point A to Point B, is 0.7 diamonds (maybe 0.5 diamond,) or a total spread of 1.4 diamonds.

Drawing 27 shows a method to calculate a shot you've probably seen a thousand times. Now that you have been exposed to these running lines, this will help you score more often. Keep the stroke and cue ball english constant.

To remember all of this is easy since you have a total spread of 1.4 diamonds. If an object ball is struck, the player must take into account the angle off the object ball to the first rail.

Review page 38 for stroke and cue ball english information.

Drawing 25

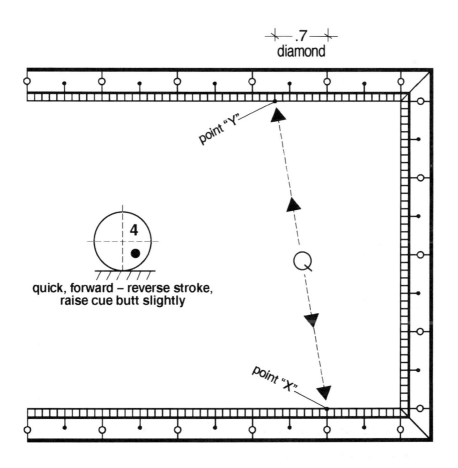

Drawing 26

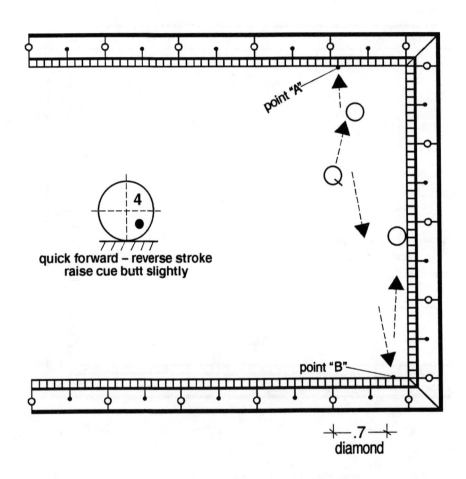

Drawing 27

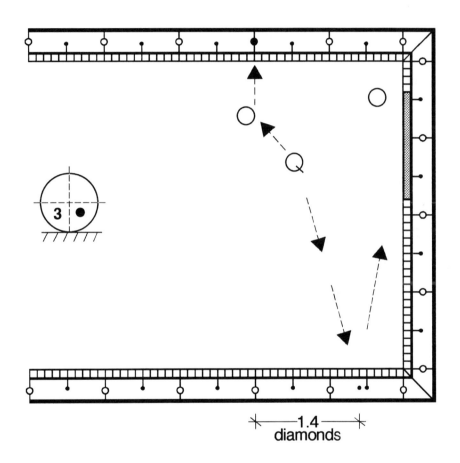

Max Across

The "Billiard Atlas II" mentioned these paths, and drawing 28 shows that when using maximum english the spread is two diamonds. This varies with the equipment. On your table it could be 1.8 or 1.9 diamonds

When the cue ball caroms off the second rail, much english remains and this is needed for the across-the-table shot.

Estimate the second-rail hit point and call it Point X. Pretend your cue ball is frozen to the "hit" side of the first object ball, then rotate your cue over the center of the imaginary cue ball until you find the two-diamond spread across from Point X. This is your first-rail hit point.

This drawing has an ideal set up. If the cue ball imaginary line is located 2.5 diamonds away from Point X, adjust the first-rail hit point by 0.25 diamonds and aim at .75 on the first diamond.

Load up the cue ball with side english, and use a full follow-through stroke with a level cue. Don't baby this shot. This has to be stroked smoothly.

When trying this shot the long way on the table, use a four-diamond spread, and a full follow-though stroke.

Test your table.

Drawing 28

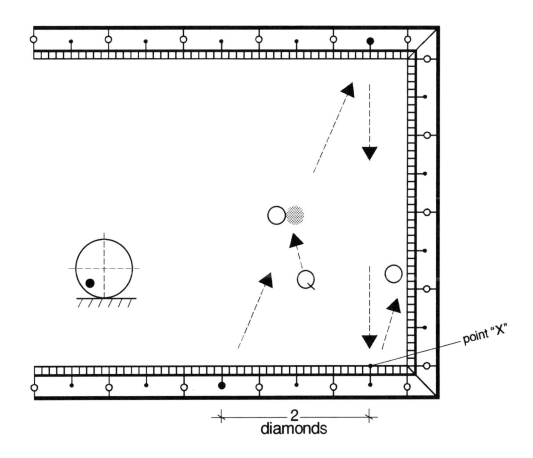

point "X"

2 diamonds

Max's Kin

This is related to the example shown on page 46. Although this is not an across-the-table shot, it fits well here.

The prospects for scoring a billiard look dismal indeed.

The triangle of lines that go from A to B to Point C, is the path the cue ball will follow when maximum english is applied, using a follow-through stroke.

This path is shown, but this path will not score the billiard.

If the estimated first-rail hit point is altered to Point X, then a different cue-ball path takes place. This estimated track shifts the triangle, which now goes from Points A to X to C, still maintaining a two diamond total spread.

The cue ball should slide into the billiard with reverse english.

Note: This shot can also be played with a jab or pop stroke, with low center cueball english. The cue ball travels most of the way with dead-ball english.

Drawing 29

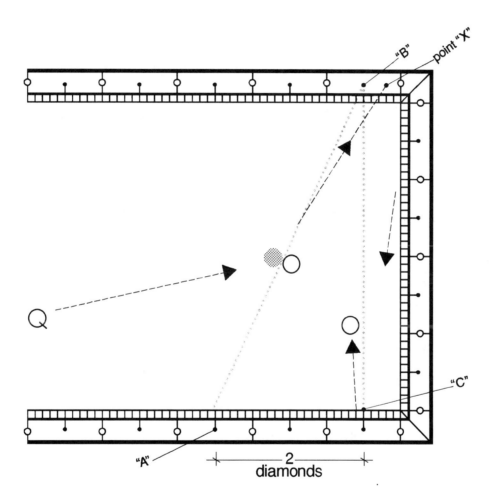

Triangulate Across

Another way of approaching this across-the-table shot is to use a triangulation system. This old system works great.

By viewing the ball setup in drawing 30, the second rail-hit spot is estimated at Point X. Imagine a line from Point X to Point B rail edge.

Pretend the cue ball is frozen to the hit side of the first object ball.

A line is visualized from the center of the imaginary frozen cue ball to Point A rail edge, then a second line to Point B.

Another line is drawn between Point X and Point A.

Find where this line intersects the imaginary cue-ball-to-point B line.

Draw a line from this intersection to Point Y. This is the new aim point for the cue ball after it caroms off the first object ball. Use the diamond mark at Point Y, and not the rail edge.

Shoot softly with dead-ball english, using a level cue & a full follow-through stroke.

Knowing how to triangulate is important. It may be slow at first, but becomes less of a problem after some practice....try it.

Drawing 30

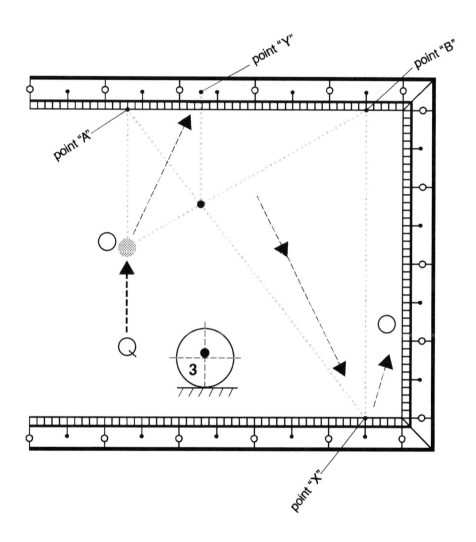

Parallel Across

Drawing 31 has the same ball locations as shown in drawing 30 (triangulate across.) This drawing uses a parallel method to determine the first-rail hit point.

Estimate the second-rail hit point, and call it Point X.

Draw a line from Point X to Point B.

Estimate the location where the cue ball will come in contact in with the first object ball.

An imaginary line is drawn from the center of this imaginary cue ball location to the desired second-rail hit Point X.

Find the halfway point on this line; from this point draw a line to Point B. This is line A.

Draw a line from the center of the imaginary cue ball location, parallel to line A, and locate the first-rail hit point. This is your aim line.

Drawing 31

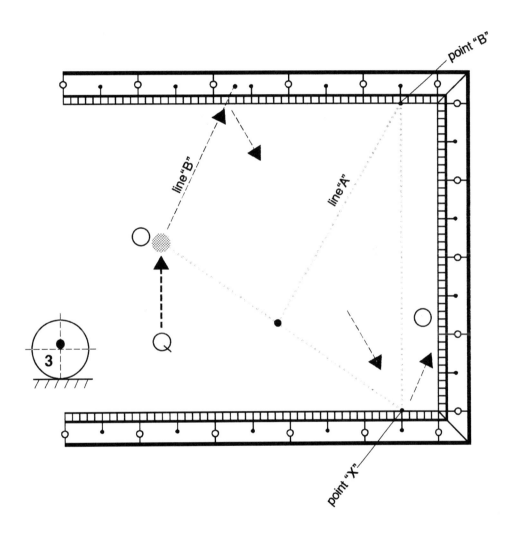

Equal Angle

The across-the-table shot is selected here. Drawing 32 reveals how to map out the cue-ball paths.

By viewing the shot, estimate the second-rail "hit" Point X, then pretend the cue ball is frozen to the first object ball on the "hit" side of the object ball.

Rotate your cue over the center of the imaginary cue ball until you find the correct angle. Have the angle into the first rail equal the angle leaving the first rail, and hitting Point X.

The path from Point A to Point B is half way between Point A and Point X. That is the new aim point.

Shoot softly with dead-ball english, a level cue and a full follow-through stoke.

This method is often quicker than triangulation or paralleling.

Drawing 32

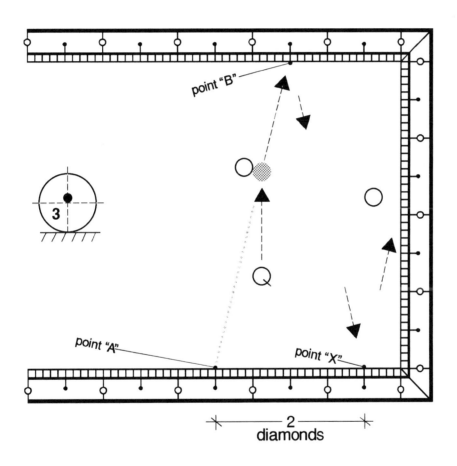

C-55

Wow's Cousin

If you refer to page 100, please note the technique regarding that particular shot. Employ the same methods for the shot pattern as shown in drawing 33.

This is a good example of how to handle what appears to be an impossible shot using the across-the-table shot.

The cue ball english is low center, and employs a quick jab or pop stroke.

Elevate the cue butt by using a full backhand grip (grip pressure may vary, and should be a bit forward.) A full hit on first object ball is needed, so hit the rail and ball at the same time.

If you think about it, only a few variations in cue ball english can accomplish different effects. Employing a little left hand cue ball english, for example, can make the cue ball come off the second rail with running english.

Drawing 33

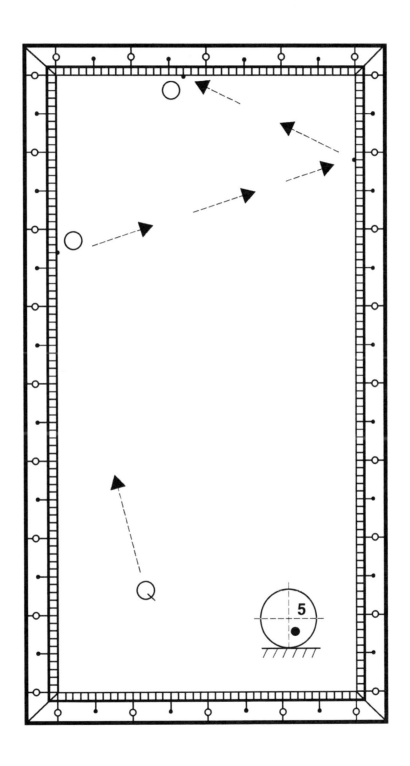

C-57

Chapter Three

Some Gems

For those of you who are uncertain how the great players have historically approached this game, the clearest explanation is from the great **Willie Hoppe,** who once described this best with:

" A pro plays mathematically by feel."

For a better insight to "feel" and "calculations," see Chapter Nine, and tune in on the mental game.

The *"Kirikaeshi System"* comes from Japan and is a first-rate method to find a third-rail hit point. A player can now learn how much to adjust the object-ball hit and cue-ball english.

Techniques usually take a back seat to systems, but they are equally important. One of the best examples of how a player can improve quickly is shown here. With a bit of technique knowledge, a common shot is tamed; see the *"Frozen Ball"* pages.

If you ever question the importance of study, just spend a little time with this chapter. Check out the results.

Kirikaeshi System

This marvelous method of making a billiard comes to us from Japan. The name "*Kirikaeshi*", means "turn about."

This was donated by my e-mail friend **Pakistani Tomoaki.** Due to his translation work, the billiard world has inherited some first-rate information.

The numbers in this technique are easy to memorize and provide the player with guidelines when attempting to hit the "inside" of the ball. The angles range from a medium angle to a short angle.

Drawing 34 has the cue-ball origin at 50, and the first object ball located at 30 (the first rail hit point). Employ "three o'clock" cue ball english.

Drawing 35 has the cue-ball origin at 45 and the first object ball at 30 (the first-rail hit point.) Use the same cue ball english.

The method of calculation, for all examples, is as follows:

Cue ball origin...minus the first-rail hit point...minus 10...equals the third-rail hit point.

Drawing	Cue ball origin	First-rail hit point	minus 10	Third-rail hit point
34	50	30	10	10
35	45	30	10	5

Notice that rail N has two sets of numbers: the "cue-ball origin numbers" and the "third-rail hit spot numbers." Observe the ever-present "minus 10."

Drawing 34

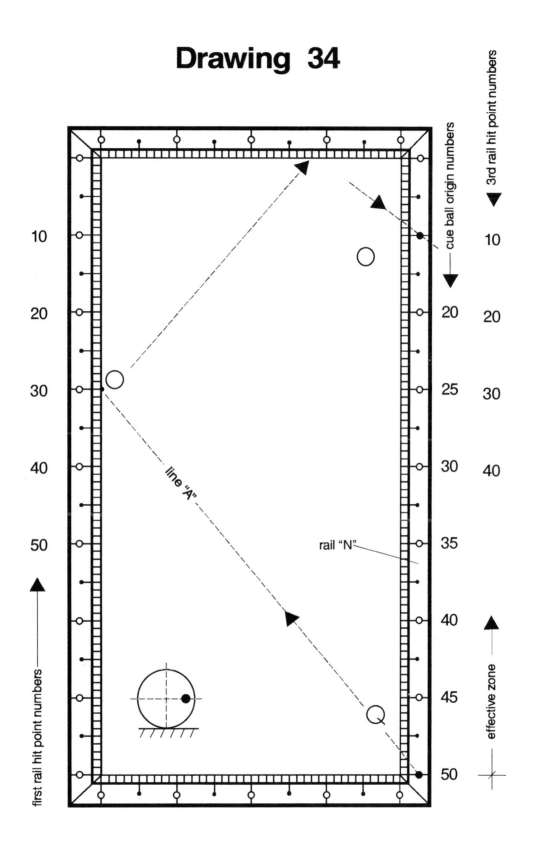

C-61

Drawing 35

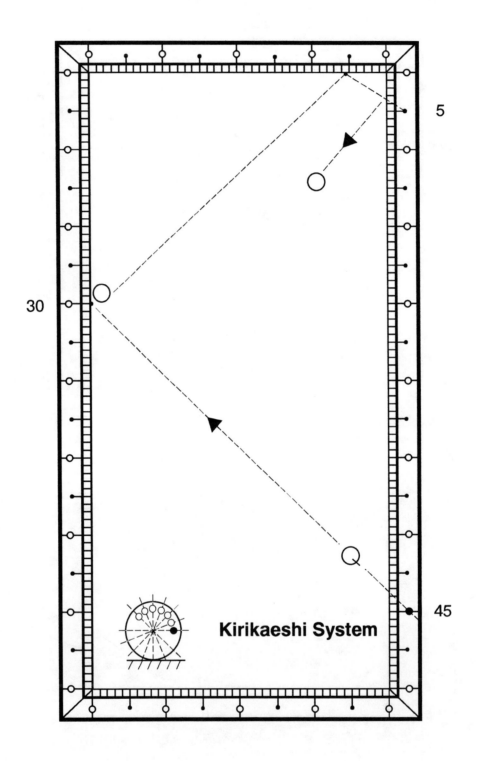

Kirikaeshi System

**Too much side english influences the path
of the cue ball, causing it to hit
a fraction of an inch away from the aim point.**

•

**Avoid extreme english.....try to keep within a
cue tip and a half, of the center of the cue ball.**

Frozen Object Ball

When the first object ball is frozen to a rail, it's difficult to have the cue ball travel as you desire. In this section you will find some guidelines. The cue ball must be driven into the first object ball with low (draw) english, so that the cue ball has a minimum of running english off the first cushion. Be careful not to over-draw. Cue-ball speed control is important, and try to avoid side cue ball english.

Drawing 36 indicates the same ball arrangement as drawing 37. These have two separate cue ball distances to the first object ball. Drawing 36 requires a full follow-through stroke and less draw english. The full follow-through stroke will retain this small amount of draw until the cue ball has reached the first object ball.

Drawing 37 has the cue ball farther from the object ball, so more cue ball "skid" is required. Deeper draw is used to keep "skid" on the cue ball, but the jab stroke will soften the draw. This will "control" the cue-ball english. The resulting angles, using each of these hits are shown on both drawings; these angles will be described in terms of a triangle. Short rail diamonds to long rail diamonds distances will be considered legs of the triangle.

Both drawings employ a one-quarter object ball hit and four-rail cue-ball speed. The resulting angles are three short-rail diamonds to four long-rail diamonds. If the cue ball speed is increased to six-rail speed, the resulting angle is longer, or three short rail diamonds, to five long-rail diamonds for the triangle. Too much draw will make the cue ball angle longer still, and our goal is to control the shot.

When the cue ball is near the first object ball, an optional approach is taken (see drawing 38.) A "quick" stroke is used, and a 1/8 object ball hit (or less) is required, along with four-rail cue-ball speed.

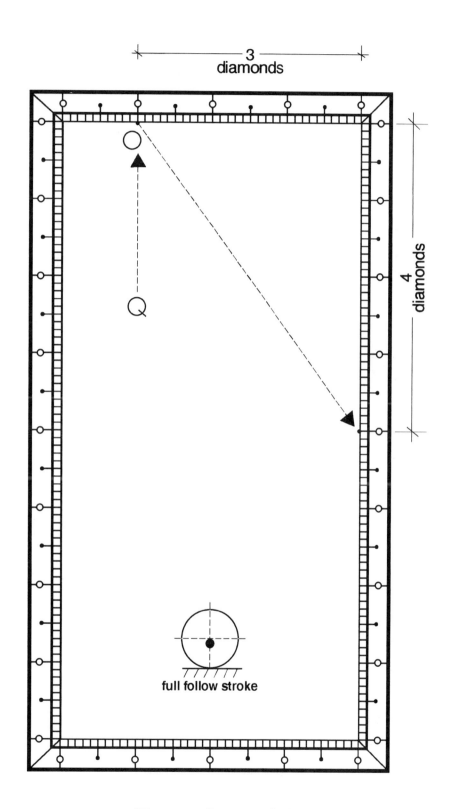

Drawing 36
C-65

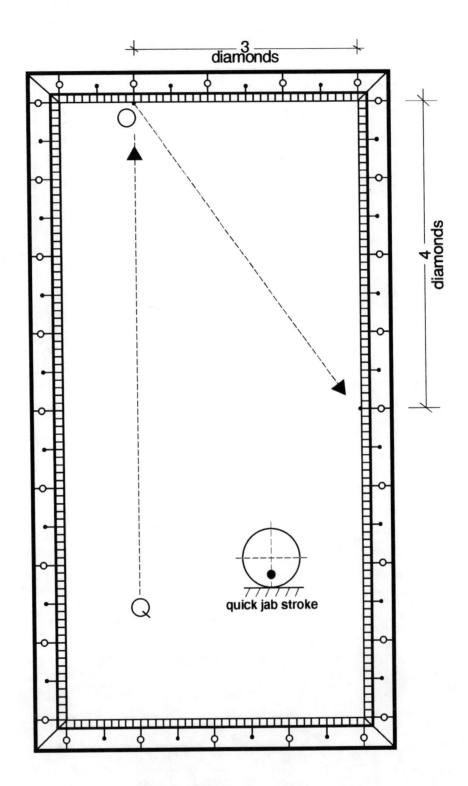

Drawing 37
C-66

Drawing 38

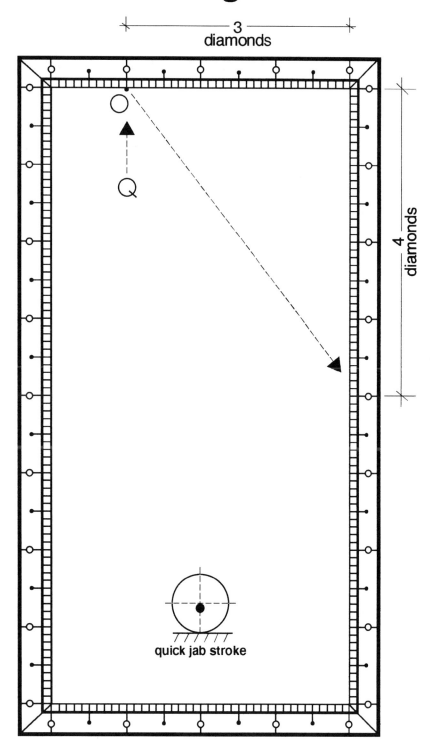

C-67

More Frozen Ball

Drawing 39 has the first object ball in a more difficult place, and a 1/4 object-ball hit would be incorrect. Instead, use the 1/8th ball hit with four-rail speed.

The resulting cue ball path has an angle ratio of two short-rail diamonds to four long-rail diamonds.

With six-rail speed, the angle ratio is two short-rail diamonds to six long-rail diamonds. Please be reminded that a quick jab stroke is employed.

With these angles as guides, the running lines can be better seen. The cue ball deflection/curve has to be checked (see page C-112.)

Too much cue-ball backspin will hurt the shot.

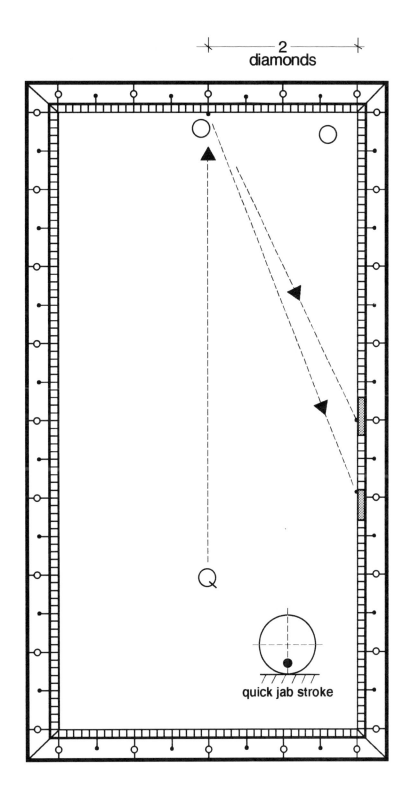

Drawing 39
C-69

Chapter Four

End Rail

Through the years, I have nearly been driven mad watching billiards made using an end-rail system, but never knowing how the shots were calculated. This is where the cue ball first strikes an end rail.

I was constantly experimenting to find some answers and found little help. Whatever these players knew, they kept to themselves.

With the help of billiard players from Brazil and Japan, we now have acquired end rail hit point knowledge. There are two great ways to map out this shot, one being the *Blue Moon.* The other is the *Blue Moon Reverse Back-Out,* and both are dead ball systems. The *Toyko Connection* is the spinning english version.

Chapter one is devoted to the study of the system in which the end rail is the first rail struck. When this shot arises, you'll be more confident. Even when you miss, you may hear a "cue tapping."

Table "slide" is an important factor in finding these hit points. Testing your table is a must.

Tokyo Connection

Out of Japan comes this obvious but elusive end-rail origin system. The basic diamond system known as the *corner-five* is called upon to help with the calculations.

Drawing 40, notes the typical *corner-five* long-rail numbers. The cue ball-origin numbers range from 1.5 to 5 (2 to 5 are shown.) The first rail numbers are from 10 to 80 (10 to 50 are shown.) The top of the drawing shows the end rail with specific numbers. Try to remember these numbers when the cue-ball origin is from a long rail.

Drawing 40 has the cue-ball origin from 5.0. If you wish to hit the rail edge on the end-rail at 6, multiply the cue-ball origin by the end-rail hit point number or (6 x 5 = 30.) The first-rail aim point becomes 30. If you wish to hit point 8 on the end rail, multiply 8 x 5 = 40. The new first-rail aim point is now 40.

Drawing 41 has various long-rail cue-ball origins, ranging from 1.5 to 5. All examples have the desired end-rail hit point at 10. Note that these cue-ball origins are all from a long rail.

To find the first-rail aim point, multiply the cue-ball origin number by the end-rail hit point number. For example, a cue ball-origin of 5, multiplied by the end-rail number 10, equals 50; aim at 50 on the first rail. A cue-ball origin of 4, multiplied by the end rail number of 10, equals 40. Aim at 40 on the first rail. A cue ball origin number of 2.0 have the cue ball aimed at 20 on the first rail.

Maximum equator cue ball english is used with a level cue. Cue ball speed is between three-and four-rail speeds, and employs a follow-through stroke.

Drawing 42 presents a path that requires a change in cue ball english.

Drawing 40

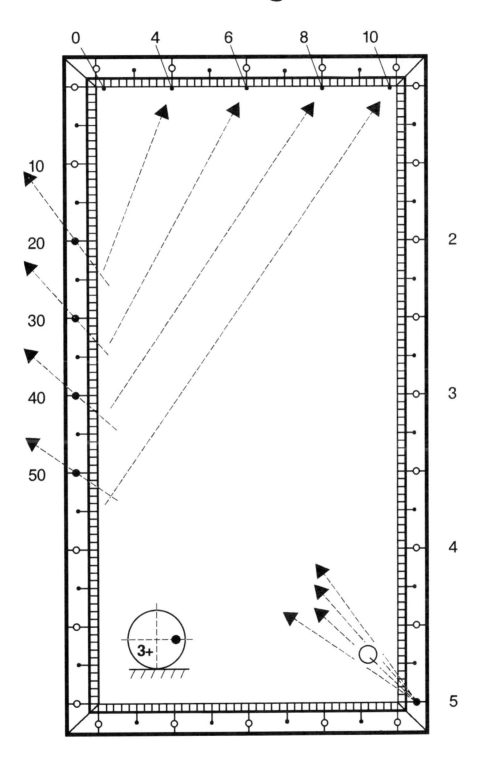

C-73

Drawing 41

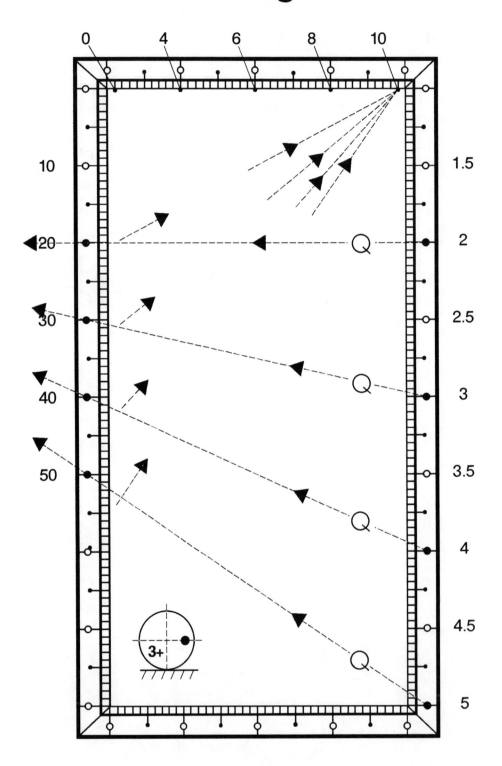

C-74

Drawing 42

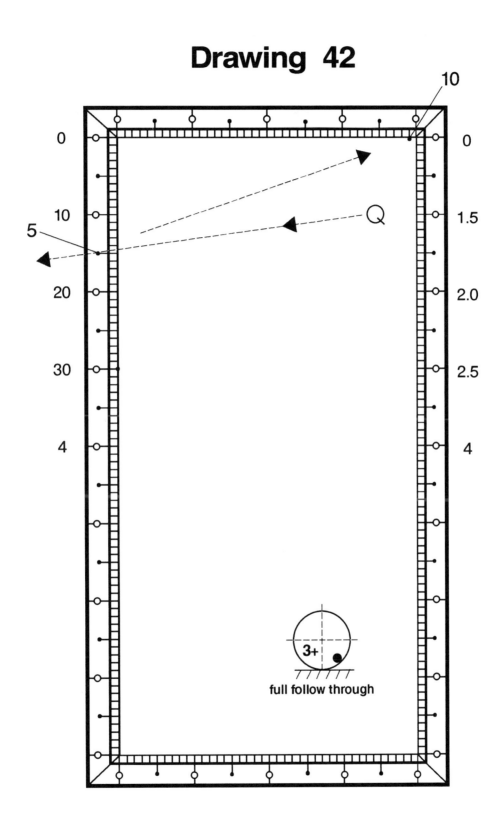

C-75

Tokyo's Change

When the cue-ball origin is from the end rail, the numbers on the opposite end-rail change.

Drawing 43 has new cue-ball origin numbers, and these numbers turn the corner from 5 and continue on to 6, 7 & 8.

All examples have the second-rail aim point at 10. The target number 10 changes with each cue-ball origin between 6 and 8.

The second-rail hit point number of 10 changes to 9.0 when the cue-ball origin is 6. The cue ball-origin of 7 causes Point 10 to change to 8.5. A cue ball origin of 8 causes Point 10 change to 8.0. Actually, it's a fairly simple change...9.0, 8.5 & 8.0.

To find the first-rail aim point when the cue-ball origin is 6, multiply the cue-ball origin of 6 by the second-rail hit point of 9 and this equals 54; aim at 54 on the first rail.

A cue-ball origin of 7 is multiplied by the second-rail hit point of 8.5 which equals 59.5; aim at 59.5 on the first rail. A cue-ball origin of 8, multiplied by the second-rail hit point of 8.0 equals 64, so aim at 64.

Drawing 44 shows a good example of having something to shoot at when all else looks bleak.

From the previous pages, it is known that when the cue-ball origin is 8, and the desired end-rail hit point is 8 (or Point B.) You find the first-rail aim point by multiplying 8 x 8, which is 64. Out of the corner at the second-rail hit point, a "whipping" action will occur, and this should have the cue-ball path reaching the fourth rail near 60.

If you score, you should hear five cues tapping.

Drawing 43

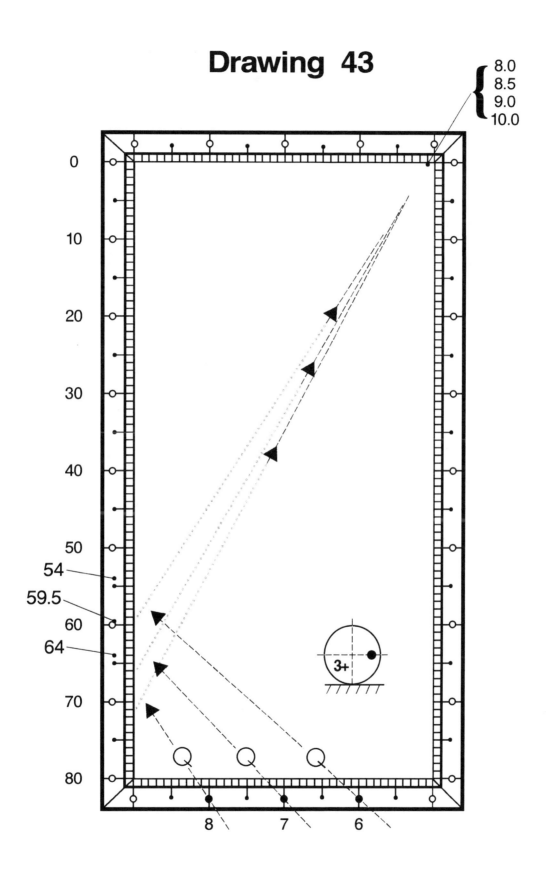

C-77

Drawing 44

If you hit the cue ball harder or easier than you intended, you will find the result to be wrong

East End

Drawing 45 will reveal what occurs when the cue-ball origin is from 6, which is a far end-rail origin.

Notice that the second-rail hit points change slightly; these numbers are shown as 4, 7, 8, & 9.

This drawing shows four separate paths using the same formula. The cue-ball origin of 6, multiplied by the second-rail hit point number of 4 equals 24. Aim at 24 on the first rail.

The cue-ball origin of 6, and this multiplied by the second rail hit point of 7 equals 42. Aim at 42.

Another path has the cue-ball origin at 6, and this multiplied by the second-rail hit point of 8 equals 48. Aim at 48.

The last path has the cue ball origin at 6, and this multiplied by the second-rail hit point of 9 equals 54. Aim at 54 on the first rail.

Drawing 45

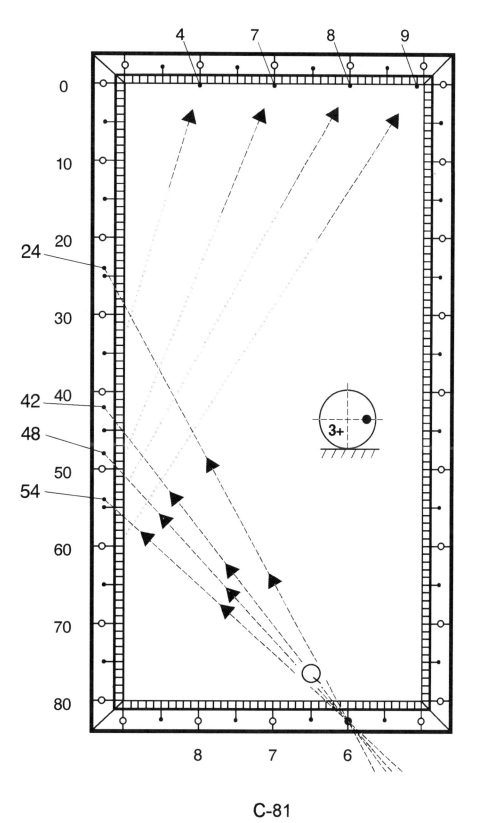

C-81

Far East End

This is a continuation on the study of cue-ball origins from an end rail with the cue ball origins changed to points 7 and 8.

Drawing 46 shows one number changed on the second rail. These second rail numbers are now 4, 7, 8 & 8.5.

Drawing 47 has different second rail hit numbers with, 5, 7, 7.5, and 8.0.

The cue-ball origin number multiplied by the second-rail hit point number, equals the first rail aim point.

Cue-ball origin	Second-rail hit point	First-rail aim point
Drawing 46		
7	4	28
7	7	49
7	8	56
7	8.5	59.5
Drawing 47		
8	5	40
8	7	56
8	7.5	60
8	8	64

The second-rail hit point numbers change, and they are not easy to remember.

Once memorized, you can now attempt rail-first bank shots when impossible billiard patterns present themselves.

Drawing 46

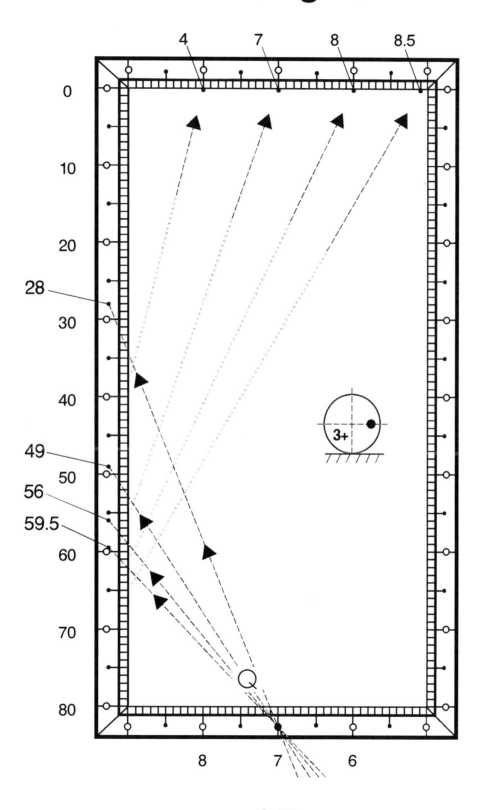

C-83

Drawing 47

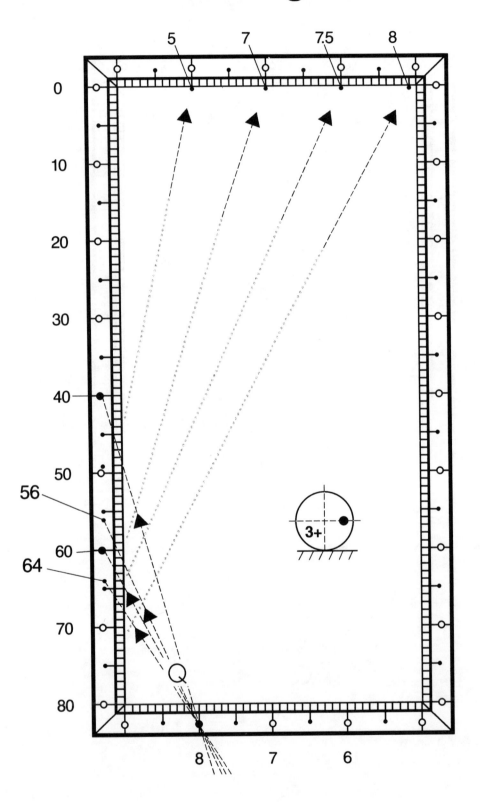

C-84

A cue ball struck at dead center, or a little below, runs more accurately than when struck above this point.

■

This is why you should shun the above center stroke.....thus avoiding an unnatural action off the rail

Grab For Straws

The rail-first bank, as shown in drawing 48, has a chance to score a billiard by using the methods shown in the previous dozen pages.

In determining the necessary path, it appears that if a cue balls origin is 5, when it is aimed at 40 on the first rail, the cue ball has a chance to strike the correct side of the first object ball.

Hopefully, a thin first object-ball hit will occur.

If you think this is grasping for straws, what else do you have?

Drawing 48

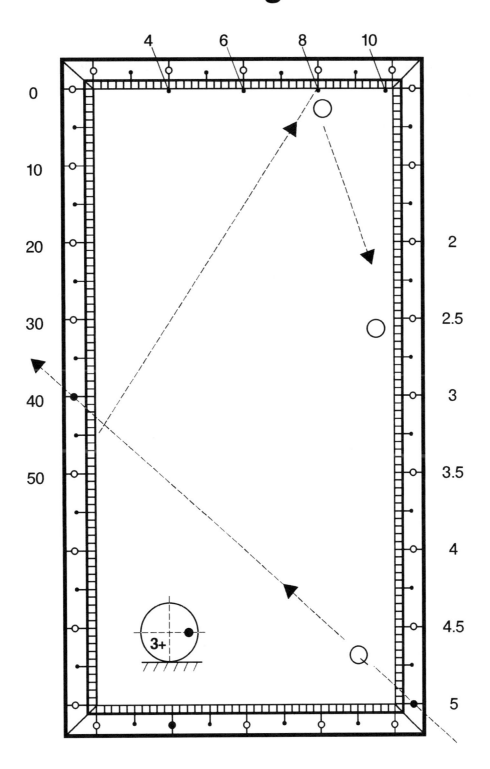

Blue Moon Shot

Occasionally a difficult shot will appear that has little chance of scoring a billiard...like once in a blue moon.

Drawings 49 and 50 reveal one scoring approach towards this billiard, and besides being viable, it has great flair.

Each drawing shows different cue-ball origins and different first object-ball locations, yet the same "formula" is used to solve both situations. Note that all numbers indicate "diamonds."

The aim spots are at the "edge" of the cushion. Hit the cue ball softly to maintain the proper angle off the first cushion. The multiplication formula is shown on each drawing.

Drawing 49 has the numerator at eight diamonds, or the long rail length.

The denominator is the sum of the cue-ball location and first object-ball location distances from the long rail, or "hit" rail. This is two diamonds and one diamond. See drawing for multiplication.

Test the table to see if an *allowance is needed*. The allowance on my table is + 0.3 diamonds. Therefore, in drawing 49 my first rail-hit point is 5.33 + 0.3, or 5.63.

Drawing 50 has the first-rail hit spot at 2.66 plus 0.3, or 2.96. If the table has a great deal of slide, try a graduated allowance. Instead of 0.3, try 0.1 from a cue ball origin point, then graduate to 0.2 at the next cue-ball origin point, and so on.

This shot is rarely attempted because missing by a mile might be embarrassing. Not to worry...you'll get a cue tapping for trying it.

Drawing 49

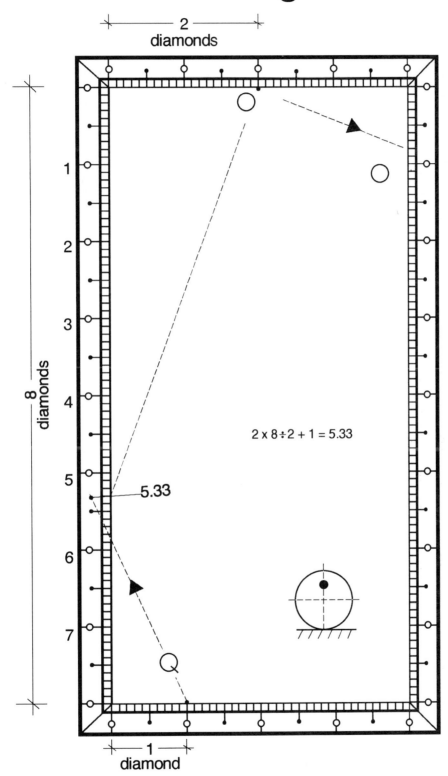

Drawing 50

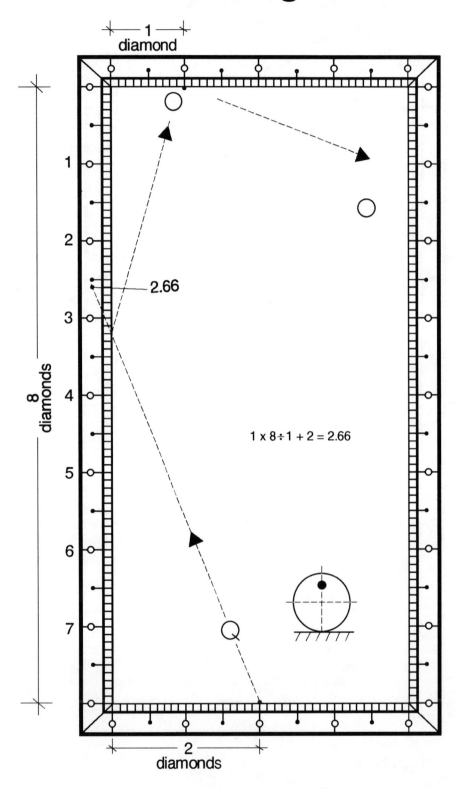

C-90

Small Moon

When the cue ball is away from the cue-ball origin rail, it is more difficult to determine the cue-ball origin.

Drawings 51 and 52 show another way of finding this cue-ball origin number, by just moving the imaginary end-rail next to the existing cue ball location.

Sometimes the cue ball rests on this imaginary rail, so the calculations are easy; otherwise, this rail edge must be estimated.

Note the numerator is calculated differently. Instead of using eight diamonds as a multiplier, use the diamond distance from the imaginary rail to the second-rail hit point.

See formulas inside the drawings.

Drawing 51

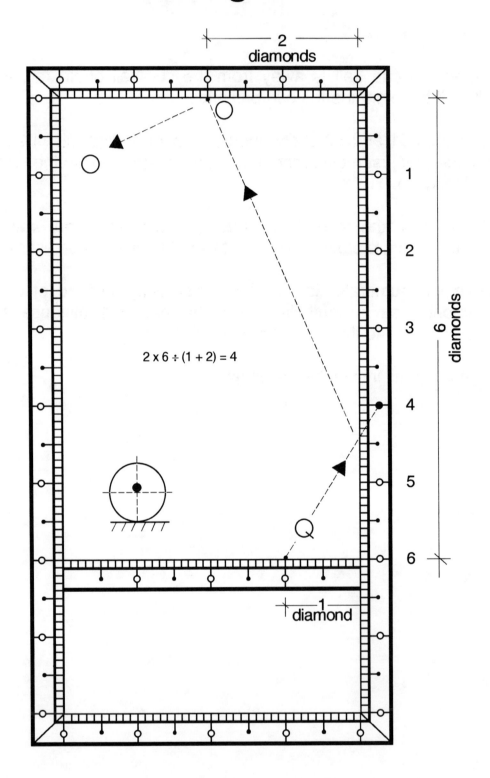

Drawing 52

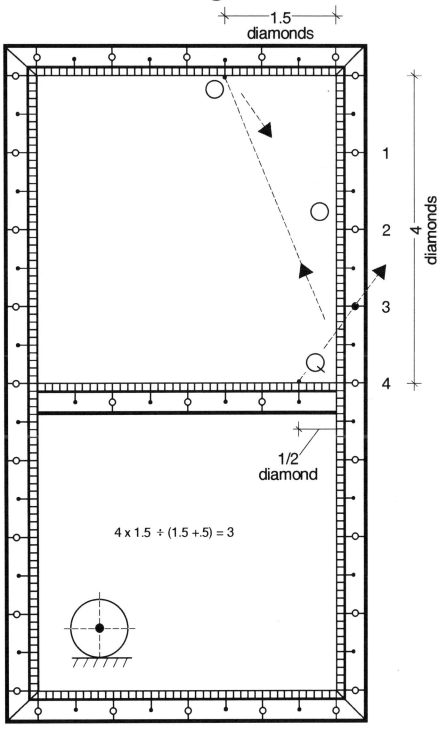

C-93

Blue Moon Reverse Back Out

A cousin of the *Blue Moon* is the reverse english version of that system. This is also an extension of the *Reverse Back Out* system shown in the Billiard Atlas II, Chapter VIII.

The formula used in the *Blue Moon* is also employed here.

Drawing 53 is similar to *Blue Moon's* drawing 49, except the opposite side of the first object ball is struck and the cue-ball english is changed.

The allowances are slightly different since "rolling" english is not used. Reverse side cue ball english will have the cue ball slide a bit, and more speed will alter the angle. Therefore, test the table for a new allowance.

On a long angle such as this, *the harder you strike the cue ball, the sharper the angle is off the rail, and the same applies for a cue ball struck below center.*

Because extra speed is required, the aim point is moved to 5.5 on my table.

Desperate measures are sometimes employed for scoring a difficult billiard.

Drawing 53

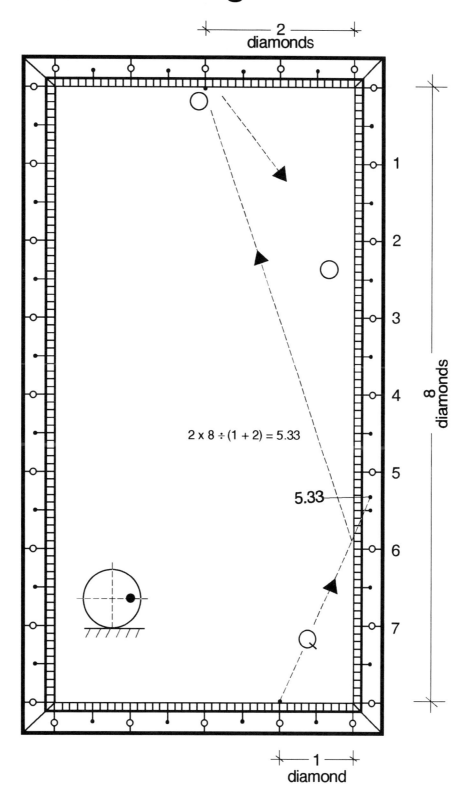

C-95

Chapter Five

How To

This chapter contains a collection of certain billiard shots that appear frequently. It is the policy of the *Billiard Atlas* books to cover information that belongs only to a "family" of shots.

Your will also discover how to avoid a kiss on a certain five-rail shot.

The *Wow* shot is one you may never have tried, but when you give this a try, you will be glad you did. We are talking eye-popping.

The *Spot-On-The-Wall* method needs more investigation; the examples shown in this chapter will expand on its use. This approach will open the door to more scoring.

Paralleling and Mirror-Mirror are two wonderful systems to add to your "*how-to*" list.

The *"Basic Diamond"* system is reviewed. The introduction of heated tables, compressed cushions and slippery balls, require more information. A fact or two, on how to best handle this, is provided.

Technical data regarding cue-ball movement is included here. It is of major importance in obtaining good object-ball hits.

Miss-A-Kiss-A-Day

This is the easiest way to map out this particular kiss...the one that shows up in almost every game.

Drawing 54 demonstrates the player attempting a five-rail billiard. The kiss is avoided as follows;

Make sure that when your cue ball gets to corner X, the first object ball will be near Point B.

Many variations can arise, and good advice is to have the first object ball travel into the first rail at a ninety-degree angle.

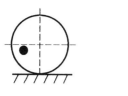
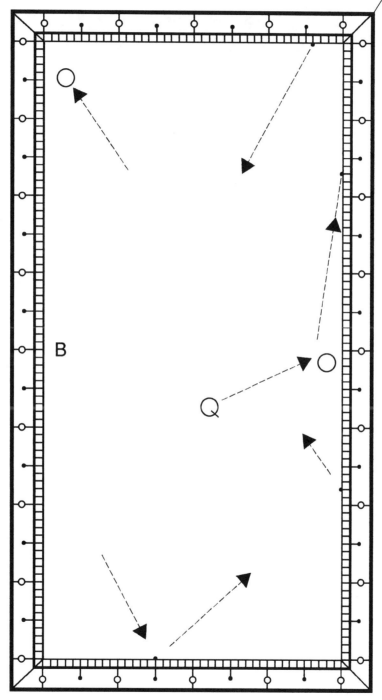

Drawing 54
C-99

Wow Shot

Drawing 55 shows the difficult alternatives the player faces. The rail-first shot will not be attempted because it looks impossible to accomplish.

Let us be adventuresome, and try it anyway.

Here are the mechanics:

Elevate the cue butt.

Cue ball english should be center and low.

Use a full grip on the backhand.

A quick stroke (jab or pop stroke) is employed.

Grip pressure may vary, and should be a bit forward.

A full hit on first object ball is needed.

Hit the rail and ball at the same time.

You'll hear a definite **wow** when you score.

Drawing 55

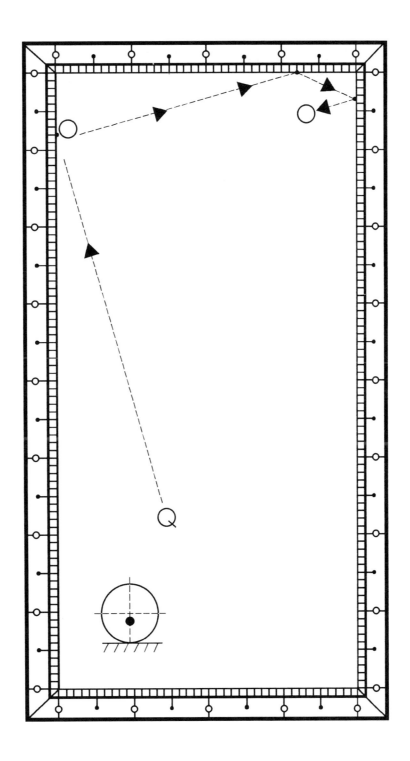

C-101

Paralleling

Paralleling is a less popular method of mapping out a shot but occasionally comes in handy. Why not know something about it ?

Drawing 56 shows how it's done.

Find the halfway point A between the cue ball and the second-rail hit point. From point A, draw a line to the corner.

Move your cue stick parallel to this line until it's over your cue ball. This is your new aim point.

Employ high center cue-ball english, with a short bridge and a follow-through stroke.

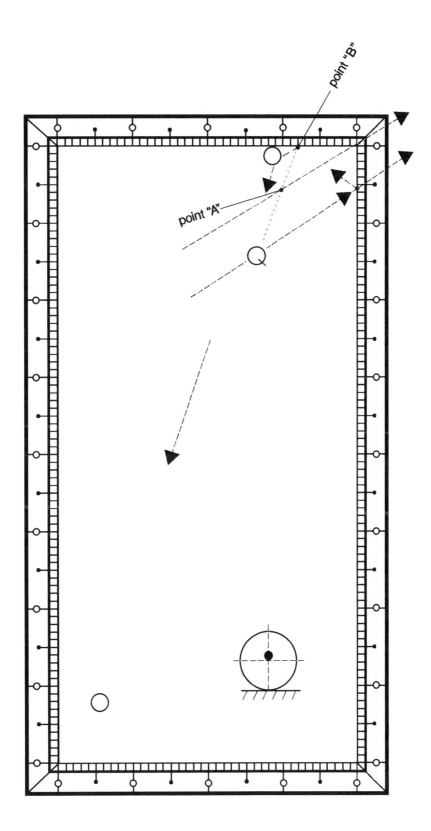

Drawing 56
C-103

Mirror, Mirror

The fact that this simple technique is unused by most players is mind-boggling. This is an excellent example of how small bits of information can pay dividends.

Drawing 57 has the player attempting a rail-first shot with a thin hit off the first object ball, then into corner X.

To get a rail-first thin hit on the right side of the first object ball, **aim** for a thin hit on the *left* side of the first object ball.

A "mirror" effect is employed.

This method opens the door to more accurate hits on the first object ball, and even 1/4 object-ball hits can be accomplished. Just aim for 1/4 hits on the other side of the object ball.

English can vary, depending on your desired cue-ball path.

" Only when the cue ball is hit softly and without english is the angle into the rail equal to the angle of reflection."

Running cue-ball english will change the hit on the object ball, and so will equipment with lots of table slide.

Drawing 57

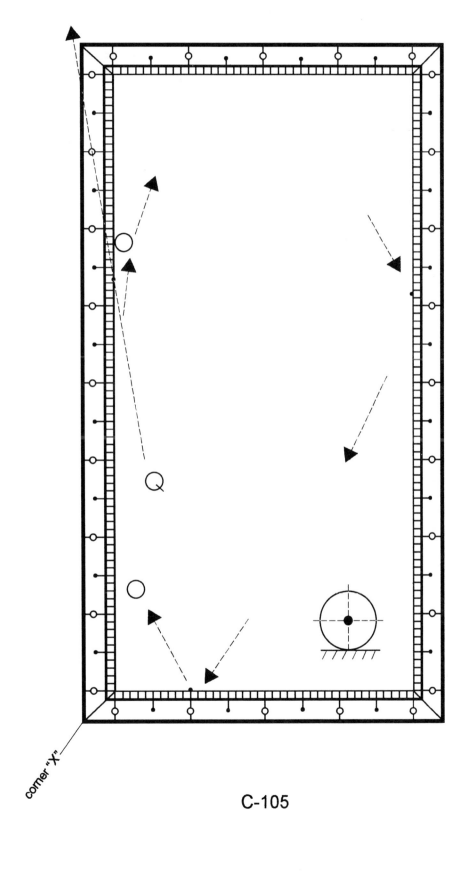

corner "X"

C-105

Spot On The Wall

When the player memorizes the "*basic*" running lines, he must then translate this knowledge to solve the problem at hand. It is important to picture the entire path of the cue ball, and the easiest method of calculating a running line is to use the s*pot-on-the-wall* method. This method has its limitations since it is employed for **three-cushion shots only**. The distance to the spot has to be somewhat correct. *The distance beyond the table to the spot is the distance between the cue-ball origin point, and the first-rail hit point.*

The drawings on the following pages reveal two examples of locating the cue-ball paths that are simple to learn. After the billiard choice is selected, then *"estimate"* the cue-ball path and mark the first-rail hit point. Call it Point S. See drawing 58.

Pretend to make a 3-rail bank shot from corner X, and assume the first object ball is not on the table. From the imaginary cue-ball location at corner X, sight through the first rail to a spot on the wall, about eight feet past the table to Point A. Mark this spot. Now return to the original billiard example, and from Point S, aim for the spot on the wall.

Use the basic paths, as noted when the table was tested, or estimate path A. To have the cue ball behave as you wish, elevate the cue butt and use a short bridge. Employ a quick ("jab" or "pop") stroke.

Drawing 59 shows an example where a bank shot is attempted, and an extremely long angle is a problem. Here again, the angle was known when the table was tested and this path is line B, which is the perfect line from Point C to score this billiard. But the cue ball is at Point T, so extend line B through the first cushion to a spot on the wall about eleven feet beyond the table. From point T aim for the spot on the wall. The distance from Point T to the far end of the table is equal to the distance used beyond the table.

Drawing 58

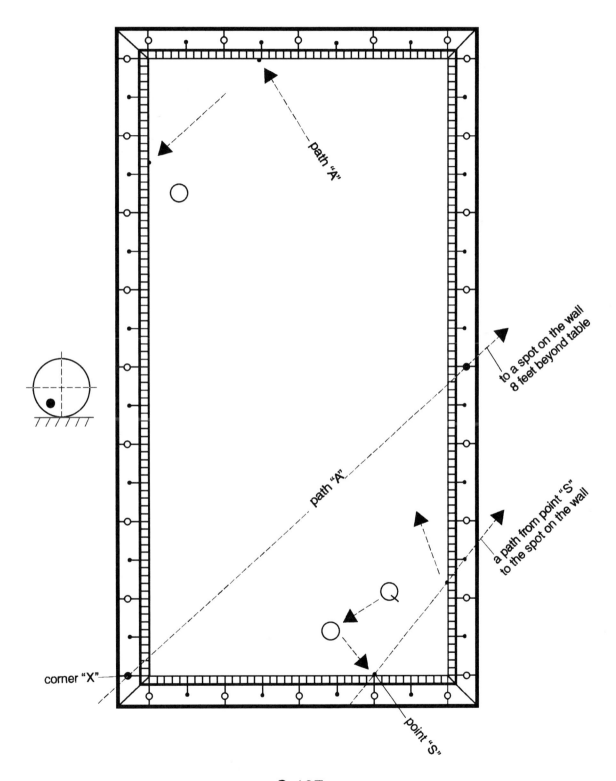

C-107

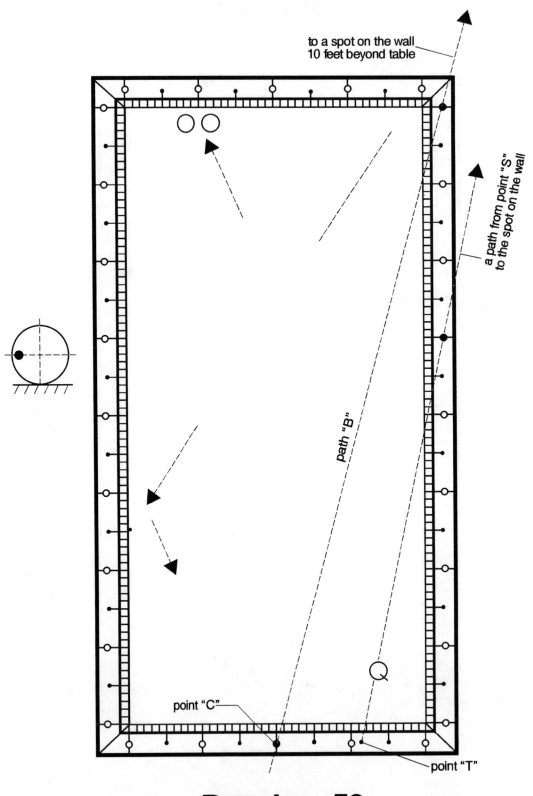

Drawing 59
C-108

Basic Diamond System

With the emergence of heated tables, slick rail cloth, slippery balls and compressed cushions, the table now plays with more "slide" and the angles become wider. Cue-ball speed also becomes an important matter, because more cue-ball speed creates yet *wider* angles. This in turn will alter the "basic diamond system" running lines, no matter what "system" is used. The running lines shown in the Billiard Atlas I, pages 85 to 133, are okay for most tables. But on a table with great "slide," a new set of numbers must be utilized. Take care with these higher cue ball speeds, as determined by checking the table. The principles and allowances, as shown in this book, are always applicable.

Don't go crazy trying any system during the break-in period of new cloth. Wait a day or so. The pro's play as soon as three hours after a cloth is installed. This keeps the new kid on the block confused, but not the pros, since they play with these conditions every week. Find the running lines for all of your systems, the back-ups, reverse english tracks, etc. When this is done, and the newly covered table cue paths are solved, you will arrive at the closest thing to euphoria. Alter your cue-ball paths as the cushion rail-cloth ages.

There are a few ways to design a basic diamond system, all of which are all complex. When choosing cue ball english, some players have the cue-ball english vary with different cue ball origins. Others minimize running english while others employ maximum side english for their hit points. Historically, the most popular system has been the "corner-five system." When the cue-ball origin is from the end rail, the numbers turn the corner from the long-rail numbers onto the short rail, as if this rail was a continuation of the long rail, which of course, *it is not.* This is where various authors change cue ball english to accommodate their own numbers. Too many good players embrace these short-rail numbers without question, and without altering cue ball english.

More Diamonds

The Billiard Atlas books maintain that the basic system is a function of the long rail, and extends the long rail beyond the existing table, and becomes an imaginary long rail.

This introduces a unique, accurate, complex system to utilize, employing with standard cue ball english in each case.

When the "Plus System" is discussed, some design their system by changing the numbers on the short rail, depending on the cue ball origin, thus they have a "set" of short-rail numbers for each cue-ball origin.

The Plus System, as shown in the Atlas 1, simplifies all of this, and is a good example of how one system is easier to use over another, even though a more complex one may be more widely-used.

Regarding complexity, some basic systems require memorizing considerable data so before selecting a system, test it thoroughly. If it's not very accurate, don't use it, but check out another. It is obvious that the extra study is time consuming, but this adoption is for the rest of your billiard life.

The ultimate study of the fine points of systems and techniques is located in **Raymond Ceulemans** book, **Mr. 100**. To absorb this material requires a dedication of an in-depth study and equipment of the highest level. The book is written in a few languages, including English; it is difficult to obtain.

Cue Alignment

Right-handed players often have their cue alignment coming from the "outside-in," so when no side cue-ball english is applied, the cue ball will "squirt" slightly. Check this out by trying dead-draw english and skid the cue ball to the first object ball. If the cue alignment is okay, the cue ball will go where it is aimed. Mine does not, and I have to adjust my hit point slightly. If the stroke tends to go left, point the right foot more outward; if it goes right, point it more forward.

A fundamental understanding of "squirt" is still unknown, but some experiments have been conducted that reveal a slender pool cue, tends to create more squirt.

If the cue-tip strikes the cue ball badly, a miss is almost certain to happen. This common problem is often caused by indecisiveness. Take extra time and be confident with your shot selection. When at the last moment, cue ball english is altered, remember that the cue alignment is straight ahead to your target, *from the cue-tip hit spot*. If the cue butt is not aligned, the player will "cut across the ball." A straight-line follow-through is a big problem for most players. Applying excessive english, causes the ball to veer to the right, or left.

Your head and your bridge must not move, but remain absolutely still until the cue ball is long-gone. By moving the head to "peek" at the shot, the player actually moves his shoulder, cue arm, and the cue tip. This cue-tip movement may be small, but certainly causes errors. Some expert players look at the cue ball last; some look at the first object ball last. If the player's basics are good, it does not matter.

The greatest majority of shots require cue ball english that is equator english, or below-equator cue ball english.

When selecting a shot, choose the short shot instead of a longer one, since it's more accurate.

Cue Ball Side Movement

This subject is about cue-ball deflection and cue ball-curve as shown on pages 96 & 97 of the Billiard Atlas II. However, the matter of *cue ball speed* data was missing, since speed has a lot to do with hitting the first object ball accurately.

Drawing 60 indicates how the "side-movement path" changes when using three different cue-ball speeds, all with the same aim point. In each case, maximum side cue ball english is employed.

Path A uses a strong-hitting stroke, with the cue-ball path as shown.

Path B uses a medium-hitting stroke, with the cue-ball path as shown.

Path C uses a soft-hitting stroke. Notice the difference in paths.

With this information, a little more is known about errors. Strong, medium and soft cue-ball speeds, make a difference. Here are two good rules:

Strike the cue ball with a moderate-to-soft speed for *long shots* with running cue ball english. With this speed, the cue-ball curve and the deflection have a chance to cancel each other out.

For *short angle shots* with running english, shoot with a moderate-to-hard stroke. The cue-ball curve has not taken place, and the hit is better.

For scoring billiards, the pros use extremely soft speeds in order to land on the last object ball without cue ball sidespin. The slower speed creates a larger target. When you apply maximum side english on the cue-ball, adjust the object-ball hit accordingly.

A level cue will reduce cue ball curve.

Drawing 60

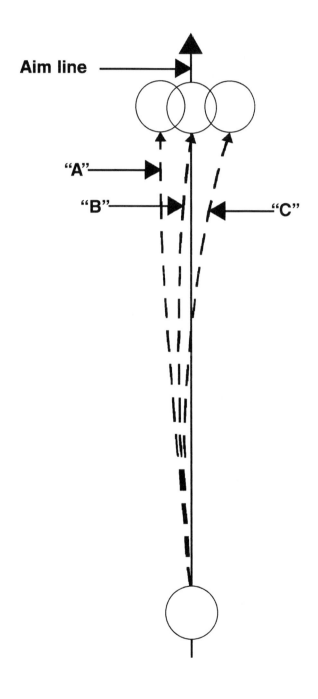

English

Good players often use cue ball english that has the cue tip near the outside edge of the cue ball, in the miscue range.

To put this subject to rest, your attention is called to Drawing B, which reveals that the cue-tip hit point, to generate maximum english, is located within the 80% point of the cue-ball width. Striking the cue ball outside this point will not add more cue ball spin.

Please be advised that the origin of this information comes from **Nobuski Kobayashi**, one of the world's greatest players.

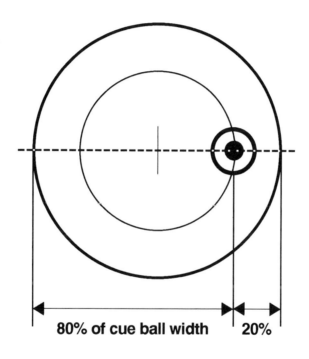

80% of cue ball width | 20%

Drawing B

Chapter Six

The Short Game

Many short-angle patterns appear in normal billiard games, especially the ones that are confined to the half-table. If a player can improve in this area, he not only scores the extra billiards, but creates the bonus of more times to shoot.

This is where the top players shine. They make a much higher percentage of these shots, and this has much to do with their high averages.

When **Sang Lee** was asked how to play a certain short-angle shot, he said, "There are fifteen ways to play that shot." This chapter will mention only nine variations of a short-angle shot.

New approaches such as *System-South, Lucky-Five, Frozen-Short* and the *Kirikaeshi* systems are shown.

A review of four other short-angle shots from the past Atlas books will also be seen, such as the very important *Ball System, Joey's System, Rising Sun and Lucky Seven.* My apologies for reviewing the past Atlas books, but it is important to gather this array, in order for the reader to be able to compare short angle shots.

The single most important ingredient in scoring a short-angle billiard is speed. It is mandatory to land *extremely* softly on the last ball. This has the cue ball with little or no sidespin, thus making the last object ball, "BIG."

Short Angles

This chapter reveals the many ways a short-angle shot can be approached when position play enters into the decision.

Drawing 62 reveals a short-angle shot that has the cue ball hitting the inside of the first object ball with running english, and the *System South* method is used.

This drawing is similar to one shown on page 2, except this drawing utilizes the "small table", instead of the full-size table. The approach however, remains the same.

Drawing 63 has a medium short angle with running english.

In this instance, the *Kirikaeshi System,* as shown on page 60, was selected. Note that the "small table" is used.

Drawing 64 will focus on an extremely short angle shot, using the *Lucky Five* method. Would you believe that a *system* for this angle exists?

Drawing 62

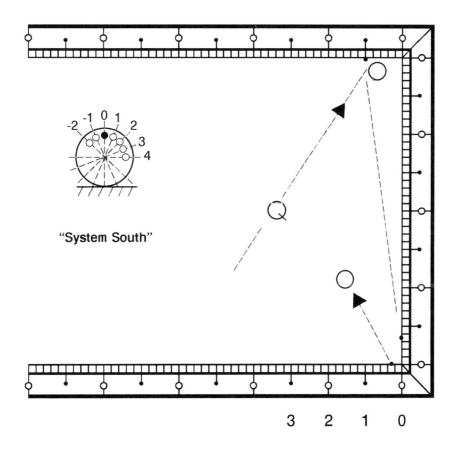

"System South"

C-119

Drawing 63

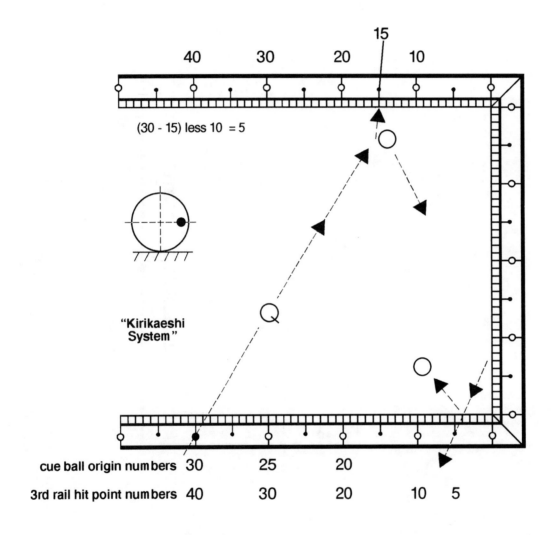

"Kirikaeshi System"

(30 - 15) less 10 = 5

cue ball origin numbers 30 25 20
3rd rail hit point numbers 40 30 20 10 5

Drawing 64

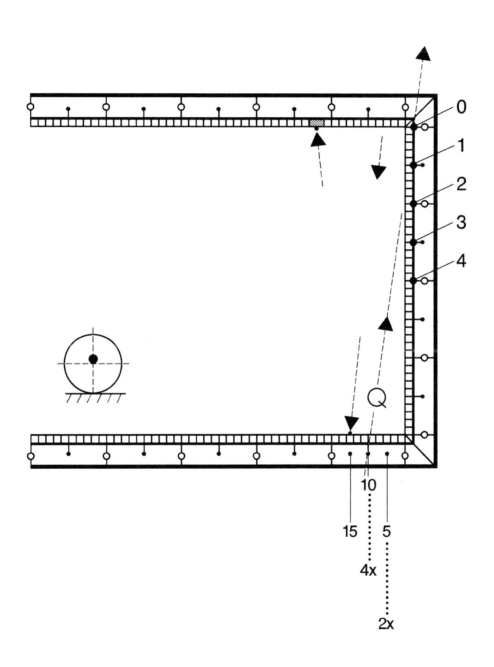

Frozen Short

Note that drawing 65 shows two separate examples, path A and path B. Each path employs a *quick jab* stroke and cue ball english as shown. Calculations are now in terms of half diamonds.

Path A uses a ¼-ball hit on the first object ball. The angle off this object ball is the triangle ratio of three half-diamonds, to four half-diamonds. Using more speed, it's three-half diamonds to five half-diamonds.

Path B uses a $1/8^{th}$-hit on the first object ball, and here the triangle ratio is two half-diamonds, to four half-diamonds. With more speed, the ratio is three half-diamonds to six half-diamonds.

You will find that path B could easily reach Point X, if greater cue ball speed is applied.

In this example, the *outside* of the object ball is hit. You could also apply this technique for short-angle shots that have the cue ball hitting the *inside* of the object ball.

With practice, you may fall in love with it.

Drawing 65

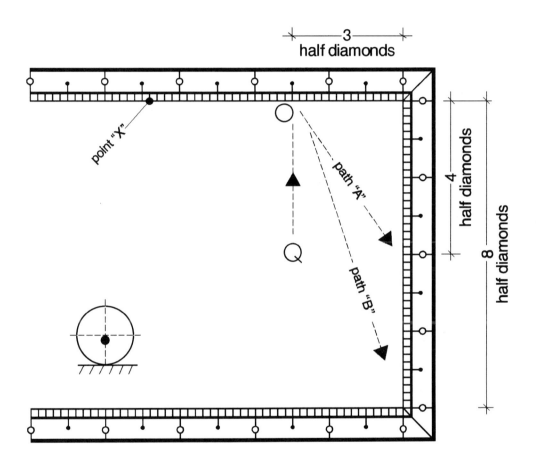

Short Review

Below you will find a review of a few short-angle shots from previous Atlas books.

Drawing 66 shows a medium short angle with the hit on the *inside* of the object ball. For details, see the Billiard Atlas II, pages 2 through 5, for the *Rising Sun System.*

Drawing 67 shows a medium short angle, with the hit on the *outside* of the object ball, with running english. For data, see the Billiard Atlas I, pages 46-47, for *Joey's Short Angles* system.

Drawing 68 demonstrates this short angle hitting the *inside* of the first object ball, and here the player can choose a wide variety of cue-ball spin. See the Billiard Atlas II, page 124, where the *Ball System* is shown.

Drawing 69 shows a medium short angle with a hit on the *outside* of the object ball. Again, reference is made to the Billiard Atlas II, pages 109 through 132, showing the *Ball System.*

Drawing 70 shows the hit without cue ball spin. See the Billiard Atlas II" pages 154 through 157, for the *Lucky 7* system, which calculates dead-ball paths.

Whew...nine different systems to handle a variety of short angle shots. This may involve a couple of months of practice, but the player's offensive improvement should astound his opponents.

A player's short game cannot be very good if he is lacking this kind of knowledge.

Drawing 66

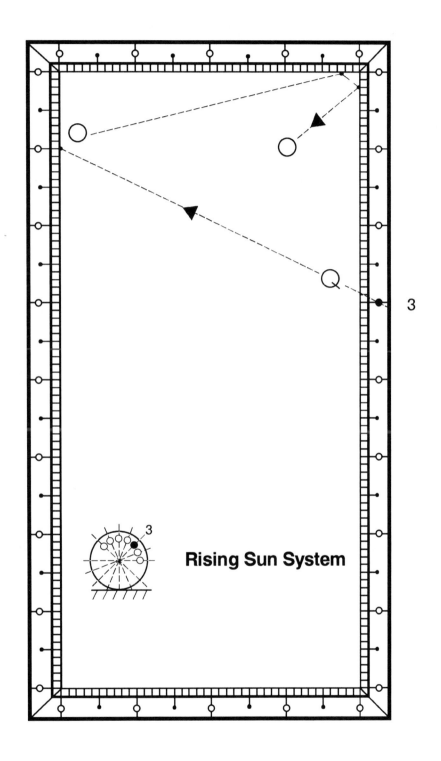

Rising Sun System

C-125

Drawing 67

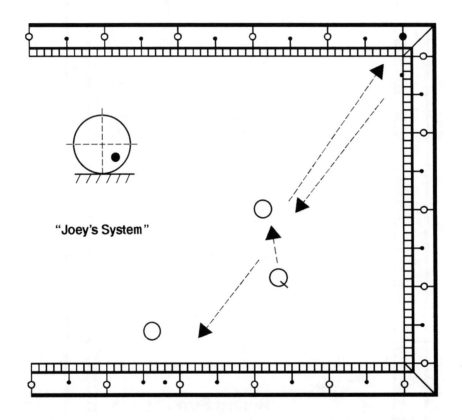

"Joey's System"

Drawing 68

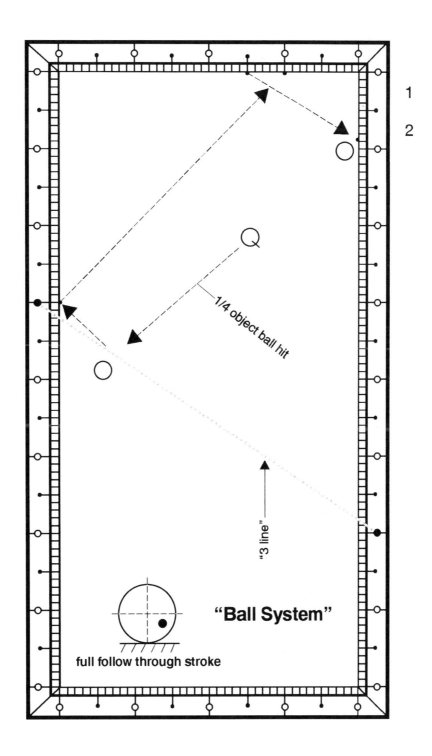

Drawing 69

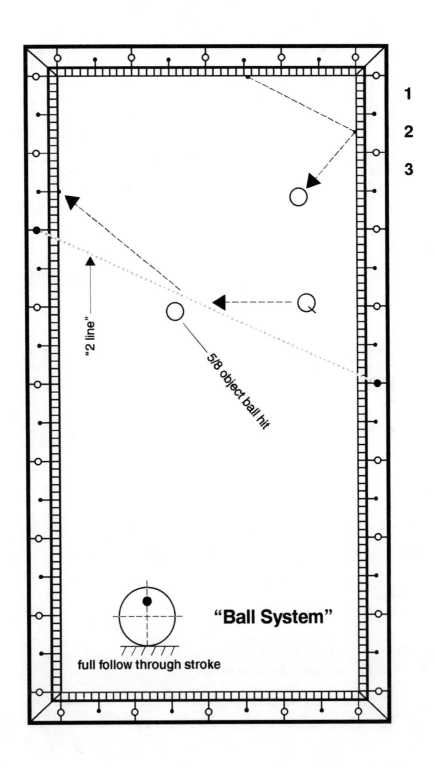

C-128

Drawing 70

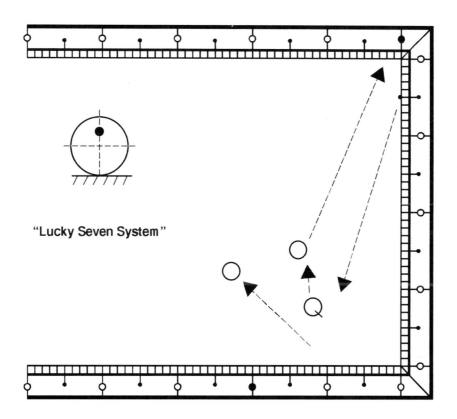

"Lucky Seven System"

C-129

Spot Check

Relying on "feel" for a third-rail point is a nice way to approach a shot; your subconscious will know the cue ball english and the speed. Selecting the wrong third-rail point is easy to do.

In the shot shown in drawing 71, the player will "feel" that the final path to the billiard is from a point on the third diamond, and this should be the target. This will be an educated guess, based on his experience. When this shot is examined more closely, an adjustment of an entire ball-width should take place.

The player must walk over to the third-diamond hit point and examine the "angle in" and the "angle out" of the cue ball. Then check the running line against his knowledge of running-line calculations. This is a case when the player's instinct is a little off, and the wrong point is chosen.

Drawing 72 reveals a common mistake when selecting a first-rail hit point. Before bending over, the player has to suspect that a corner cue-ball hit will create a whipping action problem, and that perhaps his "feel" did not take this into account. He must then go to the *Joey System* or use the *Ball System* to locate a better first-rail hit spot. He may also employ the *Spot-On-The-Wall* technique.

Be sure to walk over to that last-rail hit point for all shots; double-checking your "feel" point is a good practice. If you watch the world-class players, they do it all the time.

Dan Segal is always researching this game, and he found a method of calculating a shot that is interesting. In drawing 71, he imagines the cue-ball origin at the shaded cue-ball area, and from that point estimates the required cue-ball english, speed, and stroke follow-through to score the billiard.

Drawing 71

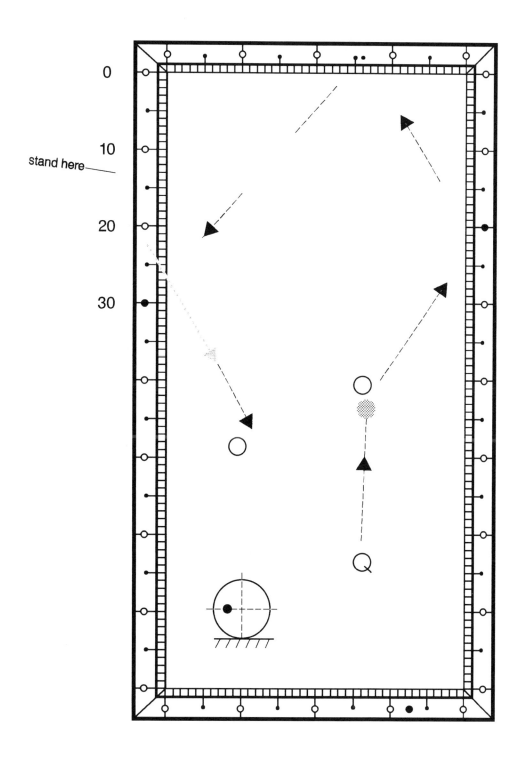

C-131

Drawing 72

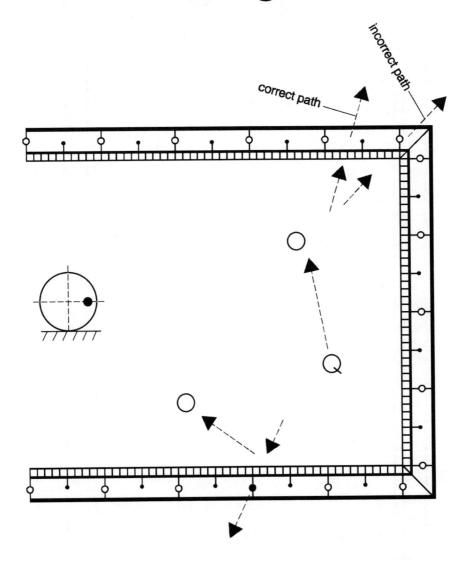

Avoid shots where excessive power is required

C-134

Chapter Seven

Fundamentals

Learning a sport without proper instruction results in the participant never achieving a high level of expertise. He may spend many years in pursuit of excellence, but may be unaware of what it takes to get better. The lack of "basic training" applies to the cue sports also. For example, a player may have never obtained the knowledge in order to hit a ball correctly. Systems are based on hitting the cue ball with a free smooth follow-through stroke…at a calculated rate of speed.

The average player does not realize that his stroke may be the cause of problems. So often he thinks his stroke is okay since he can score billiards on most shots. What he doesn't realize is that his stroke may be causing other problems and this makes it impossible to be consistent in scoring billiards. This also applies to using systems and techniques.

Too many players do not know that they are "steering" the cue stick, and this causes all kinds of crazy happenings during the stroke phase. The player may have his cue stick swing to the left or right in the stroke follow-through stage. Perhaps the cue is pulled back too fast, which interrupts the stroke cadence, not allowing a smooth stroke.

The player may unconsciously shorten the stroke length and poke the cue ball, or execute the cue ball speed differently than planned. This type of stroke has to do with not scoring billiards.

This chapter will be confined to a study of the stroke and rhythm mechanics. Hopefully, this will provide the greatest amount of improvement with the least amount of effort.

More

Once a player's stroke is corrected, other improvements occur, like better object-ball hits and better control of cue-ball english.

The proper stroke is easy to learn and the rhythm portion is also easy to understand, but both require relentless practice.

From their earliest beginnings, most billiard players are without proper "basic training." It is recommended that learning the game "backwards" begin, and a sizable portion of this chapter will be devoted to this.

Obtaining the required "basic training " is a time consuming chore, but it can a labor of love.

It can be researched through ancient reading material, such as **Willie Hoppe's** "Billiards as it should be played," or **Welker Cochran's** "Scientific Billiards."

Absorbing this may seem insurmountable to the reader, since few like the idea of starting over. When a player decides to improve, and makes this kind of commitment to his game, then learning the basics is required.

For those that want to "peek" into the area of basics, the Atlas has included many "highlights" regarding many fundamentals. Most of this material was obtained from past champions.

The all-important "theory page" is advice from the top. If you want to improve, or at least look more professional, follow these words and your game will look like a class act. Your opponents will recognize this wonderful difference in your game.

When the cue ball is frozen to the rail, have the cue tip follow through in a straight line, not up.

■

Some experts like to raise the butt of the cue and hit down on the ball......this way the cue does not go up.......others use discipline to maintain a level stroke finish.

The Magic Cure

First-rate information can be transmitted via the written word. For example, is it possible to describe a good stroke and explain it in a simple way? Most three-cushion players do not have the proper stroke, and until 1995, little has been written on this subject other than in ancient books.

In June of 1995, **Joseph Gwinn** wrote a magazine article that described, in a simple way, how to obtain a proper stroke. This billiard genius is an MIT engineer that spent 45 years specializing in accelerated motion. His billiard research centered among those champions with the best strokes, focusing on **Mosconi** and **Hoppe**. How he was able to determine the details of each part of the stroke, is mind-boggling and a stroke of luck for the billiard world.

If a player decides to follow **Gwinn's** recommendations, he will find his stroke will be changed dramatically. Best of all, his billiard output will not suffer and it is quite easy to do.

Gwinn breaks the stroke into a few parts and gives every move a description.

Clamp the upper arm against your body with a firmly closed armpit. By doing this, the elbow will not fly, and the brain will know where the elbow is at all points of the stroke.

Below the elbow, the forearm is limp. The forearm muscles do not accelerate the cue.

Move the limp forearm and wrist back and forth with the upper arm muscles (muscles above the elbow). The upper arm above the elbow should not move, only the muscles.

More Magic Cure

Keep the wrist loose, with the thumb and forefinger softly but firmly holding the cue. The middle finger should barely touch the cue with the major part of the "hand squeeze" being done by the base of the thumb and base of the forefinger. The back of the hand is an extension of the forearm. The wrist cocks easily with the hand on top of the stick, and this will cause the hand to open. The last three fingers do not support the weight of the cue. The thumb should point down, and the thumb and forefinger hold the cue when wrist is fully cocked. Minimum wrist movement is desired for most shots.

Accelerate the upper arm muscles to start the wrist moving toward the cue ball. The forearm should remain limp, and you will naturally tighten the grip as the hand closes. The wrist will un-cock as the stroke is completed, and this wrist movement is what gives the player the effective blow that allows him to put excessive english on the ball. A wrist snap, like a whip, will generate greater cue-ball effect, if needed. Upon gripping the cue butt, the muscles in the forearm may automatically tighten. If these muscles are not loose, the cue ball will be hit with a stiff, ineffective arm movement. The elbow is used as a pivot and should remain stationary with the upper part of the arm not moving. The entire stroke is below the elbow. Moving the arm above the elbow causes a "pump handle" stroke. Allow the shoulder to go limp.

After the hit, nothing must move, so imitate a statue. View the results of your shot from a "bent over" position. Try this in any game and check it out. Your billiard production will not suffer because you are *"swinging"* the cue, not *"steering"* it. This method will provide much better hits and greater cue-ball action.

If we ever get a "Billiard Hall of Fame", **Joe Gwinn** should be the first one voted in.

Note: Excerpts from a past champions writings are included in the wrist portion of **Gwinn's** text.

Rhythm

The study of rhythm serves a purpose that requires a more detailed explanation. Initially, this cadence seemed to be similar to a golf "waggle" that loosens the swing. This is not the case for billiards because it's purpose is more important than just getting loose. Below, you will discover what this has to do with the management of errors.

Mostly due to anxiety, the average room player draws his cue back much too fast, causing a faulty forward stroke. The cue must be drawn back slowly, all the way back to the desired stroke length. The cue forward motion should travel at an increasing rate prior to the hit, with care taken not to *lessen the speed*.

During the "selection" part of a players turn, the player should determine all the aspects involved in making the *entire shot*. Items such as the bridge configuration, cue-angle, stroke length, cue ball english, cue ball deflection and curve, wrist, back hand location, speed, etc. This all influences the outcome of the shot, so take your time and be thorough. This needs to be *stamped into* one's subconscious.

When the player first bends over the shot, he should check his stance, and his back arm/hand location. When the "rhythm cadence" portion of the inning is started, the player must automatically *"imitate the entire shot"* as he mentally pictures it.

This subconscious state will imitate and execute each item while the cadence is going on: the bridge, wrist, cue ball speed, "swinging" the cue, stroke length and cue angle.

If he decides on a "long and slow" stroke, his rhythm cadence has a "long and slow" movement, and the same with a shorter stroke. This cadence becomes an important weapon in a player's arsenal.

More Rhythm

Incorporating all of this in the *rhythm portion of the warm-up* will solve execution errors and save the full force of the blow for the forward motion. That's why more time is needed when bending over the shot. These *mechanics* need to be *stamped into* a players mind.

During the cadence movement, the player can now free himself to *hit the shot with his unconscious self*, thus using feel for its execution. It is not against the law to stop and stand up again when an adjustment is needed. The top players do this all the time.

After the trigger is pulled, the player must stay motionless until the cue ball stops, or at least for a couple of seconds, which is a very good habit to adopt. Peeking at the shot too quickly causes problems, such as slightly *pulling up* and not following through completely.

For most shots, the top players spend very little time in this entire process. They quickly go to the third rail-hit point, visualize the cue-ball english, and establish the running lines, without going through the steps mentioned here. They know much about billiards systems and techniques, and this is an automatic process for them.

They still take great care with each shot, taking ten to twenty seconds before striking the ball. You seldom see a world-class player take two strokes and hit the cue ball. Top players have much data to process.

Dick Jasper uses about twelve rhythm strokes before he hits the cue ball, which makes him one of the slowest players on the tour. When I asked him why he takes so much time bending over a shot, his reply was, "Each inning is important and I have to be careful not to make a mistake, otherwise I will have to sit down."

The Wrist

The wrist movement is what gives the player the effective blow that allows him to put *excessive* spin on the cue ball.

Balk-line players learn how to increase cue-ball acceleration using a snap-through wrist movement. The average USA room player has little experience in this area, but can still improve with the addition of some basic knowledge.

To obtain more cue ball spin use more wrist movement, or a quick back hand closing, or both. In this way, much english can be applied and still reduce the cue ball speed. To minimize cue ball spin, use less wrist movement.

Dan Segal studied this area and compares his findings to a cracking of the whip. "When I crack a whip, without the use of the wrist, the whip end will have only so much force, but if I repeat this using a wrist snap movement, more force will be evident."

If the entire wrist is "snapped" during the forward motion, then *maximum* force will be applied at the end of the whip. Different speeds can be applied to the whip snap, such as long and slow or quick and short, the latter is also called the "forward reverse" motion.

These same principles apply to the wrist in billiard play. **Segal** spoke on how the length of stroke, and wrist and hand usage, change the cue-ball impact.

In most strokes the maximum "acceleration force" point occurs *beyond* the cue ball's location, somewhat after the cue tip first contacts the front edge of the cue ball.

Raymond Ceulemans' best advice is to use little wrist for most shots.

Wrist, etc

If you wish to stop here in this analysis and employ the wrist snap for maximum english, please do. When you want to go one step further, **Dan Segal** offers this suggestion: "If you want the maximum force at the exact moment of cue ball-cue tip contact, and not beyond it, use the wrist snap and pretend the cue ball is at least a half-ball closer to your cue tip than it really is."

If you are striking the cue ball with more force, then pretend the cue ball is a full ball closer than it really is; this increases the cue ball effect. Full follow-through shots become easier.

Sang Lee appears to vary his stroke length each time he shoots, almost never using a full follow-through stroke. He employs many different speeds. This technique will take a long time to learn, because high acceleration snap strokes are difficult to control. Now at least, the reader is aware that these techniques exist.

Theory

"I knew the game was different", said **Semih Sayginer** after watching **Ceulemans** play in a late 1980's tournament. At that time, he was not yet a 1.00 player. This was his response to my question; what was the turning point in his career?

This was fascinating, since this led to his meteoric rise in world-class play. Yet I could not determine exactly what it was he found.

The advice you are about to read comes from the highest echelon of the billiard world and probably had much to do with **Sayginer's** success. This guide will serve as gospel for those who seek the proper "direction" for excellence in billiard play.

The primary requirements are to see the various shots, select the proper shot, and to visualize the paths of the balls to avoid the "kiss." Avoiding "kisses" make a big difference.

A player must be able to distinguish between shots that seem alike, but that need to be approached differently because of small differences, much like chess. There are many angle combinations and finding the correct path is not easy. It is difficult to establish a cue-ball location in respect to the final object ball location. The player must then be able to calculate an accurate "path to score."

Making the next shot easier makes a difference in scoring production, and cue-ball speed becomes an important item in achieving this. Say good-bye to striking the balls and losing control of them. The player must be able to use cue ball speed correctly and must know where the cue ball is going to finally stop.

If the first object ball can be positioned in a desirable area, the next shot will be easier. If you are an average room player, probably 20% of your shots are available for "position play."

Theory Continued

When reviewing a shot for the "kiss" or "position", there is a choice of object-ball hits, (half-ball, quarter-ball, etc,) and a choice of stroke techniques, (short, quick, long, etc.) Estimate the area of the kiss, then either delay the cue-ball crossing, or delay the object-ball crossing. Maybe a dead-ball shot is required, or a thin hit with a deep draw. Cue-ball speed is most important.

Attractive as they may be, try to forget about two-way shots, and concentrate on the exact speed to reach the last object ball. With this focus, the player can control the final location of this last object ball. Choosing the correct shot and not the most comfortable shot, is the goal of all this.

Once a player takes these steps, he is then on the way to being a better player. Losing control of the balls makes the above impossible.

After this process is learned, calculating a shot takes but a short time. For example, test how many seconds it takes to select an easy shot: probably three seconds for the selection and another five seconds to calculate all other factors. These top players have a great deal going on in their heads, they are usually able to process all they need to within ten seconds… and a little longer for more difficult shots.

A known veteran tournament player was once quoted; "The professionals shoot too fast, they can't possibly calculate anything." This is the kind of advice that's kept the average player in the dark for many years. The best players know the mathematics of three-cushion play because they play *"mathematically by feel."*

Position

Past books and magazines have shown the best places to drive an object ball. For the sake of those that have not seen these diagrams, let me say that placing an object ball near a long rail offers a "big" ball. Better yet, is to place one object ball in a corner.

Eddie Robin has written a book entirely on position. During our phone conversation, he spoke about having all the balls in the middle of the table, which is desirable, but the last target is smaller. His fine book goes into detail on this subject, and is a favorite in Europe.

If a person is playing pool without considering position, one has to conclude that this player is not very good or a rank beginner. A three-cushion player that ignores position must be considered a lesser player.

One of the most important ingredients in the high averages of the world-class players is position play. When **Torbjorn Blomdahl** was asked what percentage of his billiard activity involves position play, he replied, "About 40%; it used to be higher, but I was missing too many billiards."

Dick Jaspers was asked how much his game suffer if he did not play position. His reply was: "My offensive average would suffer about 20%."

I am not sure how this will help the average player's perspective, but this is how the top players operate. Not all shots lend themselves to favorable position; when such a situation occurs, shoot the most comfortable shot. Permission is granted to let the balls get out of control...maybe you will obtain a more favorable position.

When a player is in a quandary involving position or scoring the billiard, *scoring the billiard is the first priority.*

Stroke Styles

When observing world-class play, notice the different styles. You will see that **Sang Lee** employs a great deal of cue-ball spin, using considerable wrist action, full object-ball hits, and abbreviated follow-through strokes, all with great finesse.

Torbjorn Blomdahl seems to drive the cue ball into the first object ball, and is a more forceful player. **Junichi Komori**, like so many Japanese players, appears more mechanical.

Raymond Ceulemans seems to be like a machine, but exemplifies the "perfect" style, with full follow-through strokes being the general rule.

When watching **Sang Lee** from a front view, I noticed the rear of his cue stick waving back and forth, up and down, but when he strikes the cue ball, he is quite accurate. He also employs a "loose bridge" along with a loose rear grip and wrist.

Ceulemans does not seem to make the rear of his cue move either sideways or vertically prior to cue ball contact, and he employs a "firm bridge." From a front view, he looks like he is aiming at a different table.

Richard Bitalis and **Efren Reyes** both employ an extremely long bridge. It would seem that accuracy would be sacrificed, but they are two of the very best.

World-class players must all have good memories. If I had to wager on who has the best memory, I would have to choose **Sang Lee**.

C-148

Chapter Eight

The Mental Side

The lack of a good mental game often keeps a player from getting better, and is usually responsible for his playing below par. It's sad that a person can't play at his full potential within his knowledge and skills, just because he's never become aware of the mental game.

During tournaments, some players never play their game. These are the same people that do badly on school tests. It's as if some other person invades their body and takes over the cue. When things go badly, it is said that a player's "computer" does not want to accept the responsibility for the proper aim of any shot, and has a tendency to "help" all missed shots.

If that is so, the player needs to teach his computer self to stay out of the judgment of the stroke, until this need *is stamped into* the computers brain. The player has to see the perfect hit spots and execution, and takes this image from a conscious level, to an unconscious level.

Focusing on concentration does not help, because it is something you cannot force to happen. It happens when you *allow* yourself to become interested and focused on the shot. Being "in the zone" is impossible to describe since you don't know you did it until you have "awakened." You then realize you were in a different state of consciousness and mentally had become part of the table.

The "mental game" reveals that everything a player has ever learned is stored in his subconscious mind, which includes his skills and the awareness of how to play winning billiards. It no longer requires the conscious mind to work so hard, since the subconscious mind can do most of the work.

Get Mental

A billiard player's best performances happen when his responses are automatic and effortless. Ninety per cent of one's mind power rests in the subconscious. It is my guess that you have missed many shots because you were occupied with planning the shot, planning position, or planning a safety. Scattered goals reduce concentration.

The level of focusing must deepen to the point where the player "loses himself" within the game and the outer world disappears. Details are seen more clearly, and you know the best thing to do in all situations within your level of expertise. Anxiety will disappear.

Learn the correct way to play a given shot and practice it relentlessly. This has the mental computer picking up the results and storing it. Each time that is done, the brain recalls it and updates it.

Without knowledge, the player may be practicing the wrong way to approach the same shot over and over.

Your emotional baggage might prevent you from visualizing what you wish to create. Pre-judgments and concepts about "how to play billiards" can blind you to the truth.

Making a conscious decision to take the game of billiards seriously and to become a student is required. Try playing with better players to obtain new ideas.

Learning to quiet the mind is the first step and to forget about what happened two minutes ago. The ingrained mental message of "hurry up and shoot" must be erased.

These mental skills can be developed. Organize and control your thought patterns to become distraction-free. What will follow is an example of how to start. Think of your mental game as having two parts.

Mental, Etc.

The first part of the mental game is analyzing the shot selection, while scanning its data with your subconscious self, which knows exactly what to do.

You may have a talk with yourself that goes like this...find the big ball, then look for the kiss and position, then select the object ball hit and the speed. Select the third-rail hit point to establish the needed cue ball english. Check the cue angle and the kind of stroke, and adjust for cue ball deflection. Go slowly and make sure all is correct, or to the best of your ability. Your subconscious must be certain.

The second part is bending over the shot and dealing with the thought process of *performing* the proper skills. This may be your conversation during this phase: Get in my stance and check my bridge and grip. Get a proper bridge length and start my rhythm. Zero in on the first object ball hit and the required speed.

It's apparent that at least a half-dozen rhythm strokes are necessary to do all this, probably more. It would be detrimental to be unsure of the shot. If you're not sure of the shot, don't shoot. Go back a step or two...that's the way to stay focused.

Visualize making the billiard, before you play it.

Make this process a daily ritual, and do it each time you shoot. If you rush the shot, you will be unfair to yourself. You may be your own worst enemy, and can undermine your game better than anyone else, since it could be your impatience or apathy that causes you to shoot poorly. Once these tendencies are faced, they can be corrected. Being negative or having doubts fogs our vision, and these are the player's worst enemies. They make you try to control the shot, and when the player tries to control the shot, he loses awareness. When he loses awareness, he loses control.

Mental, Etc. Etc.

The player can't be thinking about how to execute the shot; he has to trust it will be done. The "negative alter ego" is a problem. Locate and control this for yourself, because it makes you miss shots.

Doubts and fears are a natural part of human life, so notice them, but only to see if they carry any truth. Sometimes doubts are wonderful early warning messages when something is not right. If that is the case, take action and adjust your creative process to keep it moving in a constructive way. At other times, doubts and fears are part of "old programs" that will sabotage your efforts.

The professionals in any sport face this situation even after they become stars, so often you will hear them say:

" Don't have the energy"
" Are not focused"
" Can't see the shot well today"
" Are in a slump"
" Are slow to get going"
" Are not locked in"
" Can rise or fall to the level of their competition"
" Did not stick to a game plan"
" Lost their confidence"
" Are not aggressive"

When you're "hot," you don't want to return to a wrong mental frame, so don't let this slip away. You want to keep the momentum going while you have this rare opportunity.

This means that hot streaks and slumps will naturally occur once in a while. Even though the player is knowledgeable of the required frame of mind, he still has to work his way out of any slump.

Mental, Etc. Etc. Etc.

Personality differences have not been taken into account. Scientists have identified a gene that influences how impulsive, excitable, quick-tempered and extravagant you are. Someday they will unravel the genetics of a personality and provide us more direct help.

It is easy to say "get focused," but another to do it. Below are some mechanical devices that will help in focusing.

When called on to perform, many players slightly tense up and without knowing it, shorten their breathing and their blood pressure rises. When this occurs, the ability to focus is *restricted*. Worse yet, the player may become self-conscious, which creates more tension. This pent-up energy must be released, so your positive energy can be devoted to the matters at hand. Breathing is much more important than you would imagine.

Before an important game, take three deep breaths, tighten every muscle in your body, and release all tightness and breath in one quick motion, like an explosion. Visualize all of this pressure leaving your body. This will do wonders for focusing, so periodically during the game, repeat the deep breathing process.

Some research now suggests that music really does help you think better, when listened to before certain tasks that involve high-level reasoning in space and time. This has something to do with the brain processes. A recent university study says, "by listening to music for a few minutes *beforehand*, you can actually prime your neural circuits and do the task better; this effect lasts only about fifteen minutes." "While the music can be of any style, it has to be clearly structured and non-repetitive" much like a Mozart Sonata or the strains of a classical guitar. When it's your time to play, your brain will be refreshed. Be reminded that a phone call, or some one just saying hello, distracts your concentration. It may take a few innings to get back into focus.

Sharking

The definition of sharking is *when a player does something to disturb or distract his opponent*, when it's the opponent's turn at the table.

It is like someone moving in a sight line when the golfer is putting, or someone making a noise during a chess game. This breaks a players concentration, and several innings may occur before he can return to being totally involved in the game. Even a phone call can set him back a few innings. Some players are notorious "sharks." How about the shark that turns his back to the table when it's your turn to shoot, and does not turn around until it's his turn to shoot? This player ruins the entire ambiance of the match. Any sharking where the shooter can be distracted is *"gauche."* These players should be horse whipped in the village square.

Once, during a tournament, I remember bending over a shot trying to concentrate on the object ball hit, and my opponent was doing his morning exercise in front of my sight line with his arms and legs waving.

In a 40-point USBA game, my lead over a former USA champion was 39 to 32 when he departed to the toilet. He returned thirty minutes later...I lost the game 40 to 39.

Another type of sharking is when the game is nearing the end and the shark strikes by starting an argument: " Three innings ago, you said you made three billiards, and you only made two." With this type of ploy, the shark shuts the game down by trying to recall the inning, and also shuts down the opponent's concentration at the same time. This person deserves the guillotine.

A parade of elephants could not disturb me if I am in the highest level of concentration, and sharking will not bother me either. At the lower levels of concentration, it's different.

When you employ extra speed, the cue ball caroms off the object ball at a shorter angle..... with less speed, a longer angle.

Chapter Nine

Equipment

Most billiard players are not in contact with the activity of the billiard world and are not usually involved in a billiard association, nor do they read billiard books or magazines. They may be many years behind in knowing about current billiard equipment or how it's maintained.

Basically they are isolated within the confines of their own billiard room, playing the same way for the past fifty years. Since then, a great billiard explosion has occurred, and offensive averages have soared.

The old Brunswick tables may be good, but can't compare with the new heated tables that are kept in top condition. Without this type of equipment, a player is at a disadvantage.

This chapter goes into great detail on "cushions," and the methods of maintaining equipment, designed to make more billiards. This chapter will help the tournament player who has a difficult time adjusting to new cloth.

Being an observer of the billiard scene, it is apparent that *constantly checking* the run of the table is required. Why use yesterday's table characteristics? This is especially true during the first few weeks of breaking in a new cushion cloth or playing with a new set of balls. The top players check the run of the table often, since humidity and air-conditioning make a difference.

When you absorb what a well-maintained heated table can do for your billiard production, you may want to join in the revolution that will change your billiard world.

The Cushion

The manner in which cushion cloth is installed makes a difference in billiard production. When observing world-class play, often a billiard is made that has the cue ball going very long. This shot could not have been made on my Wilhelmina Table, but the video was on a Wilhelmina. How could the cue ball path get so long?

The table mechanics in the USA were lacking the information on how to cover tables. European tables played differently.

This all changed just prior to **Sang Lee's** 1994 USA tournament, when he imported a European table mechanic to recover the tables properly. Two USA mechanics were present.

The cloth around the cushion was wrapped tightly so as to slightly depress the rubber nose, about 2 mm. The bed cloth was stretched to an absolute maximum, and the difference in play was impressive.

The table became faster, and the cue ball caromed off the cushions without losing much speed. It became clear that something was indeed different, so the player needed to adjust his calculation. Simple shots became complicated. Cue ball speeds became critical, because as the cue ball speed increased, the carom angles off the rail became longer.

It became clear how a world-class player scores those very long angles shots…ones the ordinary player would not attempt.

After caroming a few rails, a significant amount of spin remained on the cue ball. The spin seemed to automatically present itself, even though it may have not been desired. Cue-ball english, off the first cushion was different, and provided more spin than ever before. Back-ups became sharper.

More Cushion

With new cloth, table slide is another big difference. After a couple days of play, the table settled down: slide became more normal. A few months later, the pronounced slide was gone.

To help in understanding the importance of table slide, an example is shown on drawing 73. In this example, path "B" uses a new cue ball, new Simonis 300 cloth, and cushion cloth installed as mentioned above. Cue-ball english, and stroke were all maximum, with seven-rail speed.

Path "A" is the same as above, except in this case the cushion cloth was installed without depressing the rubber and had some wear.

Notice the difference when longer angles are available. This *"new"* table allows the player to score more billiards.

For the first five to six hours of play on new cloth, the cue ball will wildly carom at unpredictable angles. Until the rail cloth is broken in, don't go crazy trying to calculate anything.

This entire section covering *"The Cushion"* is long winded, because so much of the billiard world is not well informed about this subject. Scoring more billiards is the name of the game.

Now, the "feel" is changed. A player must re-learn the table...sad but true.

One of the USA's best players, when asked about European tables, lamented that it will take years for him to get familiar with these tables, while the Europeans have enjoyed these conditions for so many years.

Drawing 73

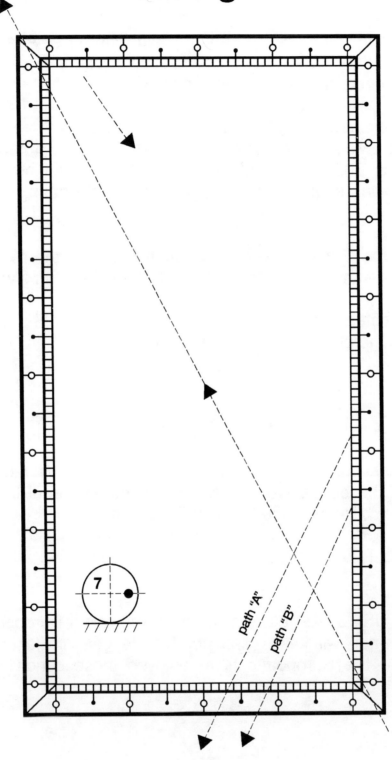

C-160

*The only time to think about the second object ball,
is when you are lining up the shot and getting your aim*

More Cushion Etc

World-class three-cushion tournaments have the best equipment and this sets the standard for championship play. When tournament play begins, players readily remember the playing conditions. During their first game or so, they are never too far away from the correct feeling and the needed adjustments.

During the first day of the contest, the table will start playing "shorter" and will change slightly every few hours. The world-class player is quite familiar with these characteristics and constantly adjusts. Not only does the cushion cloth shorten, but the new balls change also, constantly shorter.

Players who are not on the professional tour are at an enormous disadvantage when confronted with this situation. After all, how often do they play with these conditions…once day a year? Their only choice is to enter the tour without the experience of having played under these conditions.

After the tournament is over, the Simonis 300 cushion cloth will become shorter over a period of a few months. The slide will diminish and the table will become unsuitable for tournament play. Cushion cloth should be changed at least twice a year.

Drawing 74 reveals the difference in running lines when the variables are introduced. Again, we are examining the long table slide.

Paths A, B, C & D indicate how cushion wear changes the slide angle. All examples have tables fitted with Simonis 300 cushion cloth, the cushion edge slightly depressed, and a new set of balls.

Path A is from a new, unused cushion cloth.
Path C is from a cushion cloth that has one day of tournament play.
Path B is from a cushion cloth that has been used for one week.
Path D is from an older cushion cloth.

Drawing 74

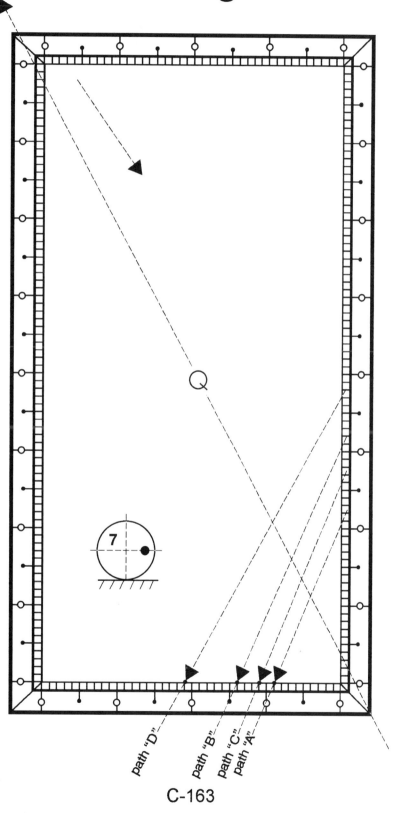

path "D" path "B" path "C" path "A"

C-163

More Cushion, Etc. Etc.

The average European tournament player in normal play, prefers a longer slide than the *worn* 300 cloth, so a *Simonis 585* cushion cloth is often substituted. This cloth does not have the slide of the "new 300," but this durable 585-rail cloth remains "long" for a longer period of time, thus allowing for lower costs in maintaining the table. After all, you can't change the "300" cushion cloth every two months, as it would be too costly. With this, the 585-rail cloth satisfies the average tournament player.

Richard Bitalis, playing in his local room in Cannes, changed the rail cloth on a regular basis, but not the bed cloth and also kept slide on the balls. New balls were expensive and this provided him with playing conditions that were similar to world-class tournament play, without costing the room owner a great amount of money.

In the USA, too often the rail cloth becomes worn or gummy from the wrong ball wax, and the slide is not evident. The room owner often does not realize the importance of slide. Most room players do not want to adjust to proper playing conditions, since winning a game is more important than game excellence.

Drawing 74 shows the problems the average player faces when playing conditions are different. So often, USA tables have path "A" or path "C" as the playing condition. The average contestant has been playing on tables where the conditions are similar to path "D", or worse, and there is no way he can play his normal game to succeed. The experienced tour player better adapts to this.

During **Sang Lee's** 1994 New York tournament, the tables played like path "A", perhaps longer, because of his ball treatment. Everybody else including the world-class players struggled for a couple of days until the table settled down. In the prelims, all complained that whatever ball polish **Sang Lee** was using, made the balls slide more than they were desired.

Cushion End

After a couple of days the table paths shortened slightly. The table then became perfect for top-level play and established new records. Too many top USA players did not reach the finals due to this long slide which, in the first two days, had the break shot being hit with dead-ball english.

During **Sang Lee's** 1995 New York tournament, the table conditions were changed. New cloth was not installed, and cue-ball treatment was a bit different. This is not to say that the playing conditions were not okay...they were excellent, but without the slide of the 1994 tournament. The general USA average for the 1995 affair was better than ever.

Oddly enough, too many so-called "good" room owners will allow the cushion edges to get worn and dirty. They often say, "After all, my room players haven't complained," or, " It's good enough."

There are many room owners that still have tables with cushions that lost their elasticity seventy years ago. These cushions have been around much too long and it is time the room owners be taken into the street, read their rights, and shot at sunrise.

If we are to breed players that can compete internationally, the least we can do is to have proper table conditions. The average room player will eventually get accustomed to this. The owner should replace the bed cloth twice a year, and rail cloth more often. Then provide players with vacuum cleaners, ball polishers and table covers, all of which will cost about 30 cents per hour. A much-needed player revolt may provide "class" billiards.

The Ball

As an observer of the billiard scene, it is apparent that much has been done to make the table as fast and as long as possible, with the sole purpose of scoring more billiards. Why hasn't more importance been given to the study of billiard-ball care? It is possible that this has been overlooked for the past few decades.

The world-class players, practicing in their homerooms, will apply their potion to have the balls resemble new balls. The problem with most treatment products is they wear off quickly, usually after only a forty-point game. It also deposits a residue on the edge of the cushion and on the cue tip. Ugly rail edges are often seen in some of the busiest rooms in the USA. Let's not forget and too many miscues.

The room owners of Holland admit to cleaning the balls with a damp cloth and buffing them dry. Whatever they use is not public knowledge, and their table rail edges are well kept.

I have experimented with a number of liquids and have found few that will stand the rigors of a sixty-point game. The hunt for something of better endurance continued, and this led me to a chance happening.

My local watering hole in Cocoa Beach, Florida, is a gathering place for NASA space center personnel, who often converse about the activities of their work. On one occasion they mentioned the liquid that is used on the shuttle's nose cone to reduce friction. Naturally, this coating was obtained and applied to billiard balls.

Using mineral spirits, the older balls were stripped of all previous coatings. A few coats of this material were applied and the balls became similar to new balls, fresh out of the box. They traveled a longer distance and had the slide of a new ball, leaving no residue on the leather tip or the cushion edge. Your can find this product "Liquid Glass," in your local automotive store.

Ball Etc

The liquid ball coating, "Liquid Glass," made its maiden appearance in a 1995 tournament in Boca Raton, Florida. Top of the line Arimith balls were used. The Sogard tables were covered with Simonis 300, and the cushions were covered properly.

The room owner was self-conscious about his tables playing short. In a test, he was introduced to this liquid coating and was impressed, though reluctant to use anything new, since so many top players were present. The first day of the contest had the angles slightly shortening. The new balls, which had many factory coats of silicone, were being coated with the usual wax between games. Halfway through the second day, the balls had shortened quite a bit, but the top players knew how to handle this, being very aware that this occurs.

The room owner did not like the short angles appearing that soon, so at noon of the second day, he used this new ball coating without telling anybody. Immediately, the billiard balls reverted to new ball playing conditions, which produced a problem for a few top players. They were expecting a gradual shortening of billiard play, and did not anticipate the longer ball slide would reappear. **Carlos Hallon** never did recover, missing many a billiard by a few millimeters. **Sang Lee** adjusted quickly. The room owner loved it since his tables now played respectably long. The balls shortened as play went on, and had to be coated again after forty points. This incident offers good advice to the student. It is mandatory to adjust to this constant ball change, and here is where "feel" plays an important part.

If the balls are heated, they will travel a longer distance. The balls should be placed overnight in a cradle on the heated table.

Billiard balls should play the same wherever the game is played, but do not. A Three-cushion player should be allowed to use his own private cue ball.

Chapter Ten

Misc.

I was a referee in a **Raymond Ceulemans** exhibition in 1978, in which he averaged a whopping 1.6 against a field of the best Chicago-area players. After this, he made himself available for questions about any aspect of the game. He emphasized that all the power he needed, he got from his hand.

His generosity in offering advice was always present, but his data was too much for that small band of hardy fanatics to absorb, who did not realizing the importance of what he was saying.

It would be nice if information and coaching came from a world-class teacher. In the USA, we only have **Sang Lee**.

Meanwhile, if a player makes a study of this game, takes instruction from our past champions, and studies with dedication, he could contend. Some of our top players are good teachers, and with tournament exposure against top-level play, a student could become a dangerous competitor.

Efren Reyes might be one of the world's best balk-line players, even though his forte is pocket billiards. Ten years ago, his three-cushion game was almost at USA championship level.

This chapter touches on a couple of areas, such as the need for quality coaching worldwide. Also included is a great idea on obtaining sponsors to provide the prize money needed to elevate our beloved billiard game.

A Survey

When up and coming USA players **Sonny Cho** and **Carlos Hallon** were asked, "What do you think is the most important single item for your future advancement?"...the reply was "Playing in world-class competition."

When I asked **Mazin Shooni** the same question, he said: "Stroke knowledge," which indicates the need for quality instruction.

These remarks come from players averaging above 1.00 and looking to improve their game. If you are lucky enough to play with high-caliber players, it is obvious that your offensive average will improve, because you will be able to observe shots played properly. It will be easier to see when a jab shot is employed, to see the care these players employ, or how they select shots so their position is better. If something needs clarification, they may discuss it with you after the game.

During the past twenty years, **Raymond Ceulemans** paved the way for world-class billiard players. Top international players were able to advance because of his knowledge and today's higher averages resulted.

Coaching

Shown below is an interesting editorial on coaching from the "World Report 3-Cushion" magazine. This is an altered summary of it.

••••

Most sports have a trainer, or a coach at their establishments, or clubs, who try to teach members the finer points of the game, but not in billiards. The average room player has his weekly game and that's about it. He might get some minor tips or instructions by fellow members.

Fanatics, who want to invest in their game, will arrange for lessons. Those who don't have the required money will muddle along, and their game will not improve at all. Since the game was organized some eighty to ninety years ago, hardly anything has changed, so when do we wake up?

If clubs or billiard rooms would recruit a coach, or trainer, as in other sports, the level of play would rise and concerned players would start to enjoy their game. The less talented player will be able to make progress from say an approximate .300 to .500 average, or from an approximate .500 to a .800 average, not to mention the tremendous kick one gets by passing the 1.00 barrier.

The billiards community has been taken for granted for too long. Nobody has ever given attention to the technical aspects of this game, nor the mental aspects. We must change the game so it becomes a respected sport, which would create interest in all levels.

It would be wonderful if the average players would not only play their normal games, but would have the opportunity to be taught each week. Too many years of neglect have gone by; perhaps now, we can change all this.

USA Tournament Formats

When the international tournament formats went to fifteen-point games, **Raymond Ceulemans** was at a loss. He was the best, so why should he have to endure fifteen point games? The reason was that this created more interest, and the game fared better.

Our formats have not changed in forty years; we still have tournament formats that smack of the 1950's. It is common to see a weekend tournament where the player is expected to play 280 points on Friday night and Saturday. If he makes the finals, he must then play 280 points on Sunday. His first game may be at 9:00 a.m., and his last at midnight. The quality of billiard expertise suffers. Who wants to muster up the required concentration for this long of an ordeal? Then we have the player that works on Saturday or evenings, or have pending family matters, or other pursuits. There is also the older player who cannot endure these marathons. All of the above has to do with tournament interest. When the fathers of this crazy scheduling are approached for some accountability, they appear open-minded, innocent and quizzical, but below that facade, lurks "billiard insanity." Nothing ever changes. It is obvious that this type of attitude is slanted towards ancient thinking, with the prize money going to the same players...the regulars or the good old boys. If change is to occur, more interest has to be generated for the majority of players.

There are not enough tournaments, and for the few that do occur, the entry fee is too large. As of this writing, we do not have a two-man, or four-man team tournaments, or senior contests. Encouraging a two-person entry would alleviate some of the above problems. Fifteen-point tournament games are rarely played in this country. Probably the greatest injustice done to our USA billiard world is not to maintain rankings, and we may be the only country that does not. For the present, governing bodies *ignore publishing* data of how one player rates against the others, and that is unforgivable.

Fifty Innings

Late last year, a new type of competition called the **ladder club** began in Chicago, creating plenty of excitement. This simple format has the player in a fifty-inning game. After three games his average is determined, then he is ranked. Once a player is ranked, he can improve his standing by challenging one of the next two players that rank directly above him. If the lower ranked player wins a match, the players exchange positions on the ranking ladder. When the higher player wins, they retain their previous ranking. The difference between two players ratings is the handicap that the lower player receives in a match.

Forty players signed up for the first tournament, and it was extremely popular. Presently, at Chicago's **Chris's billiards,** there's a waiting list for the next set of matches. Tournaments are scheduled continuously throughout the year, and the formats vary. Each player schedules his own matches, usually by phone, so he can play when it's convenient.

The official rules are established, and here are some of the features; Ladder matches take precedence over open play. The player's scores are constantly averaged and multiplied by 80% to arrive at a ranking. A limit of forty players was established for four Verhoven tables. Twenty matches per week has been the average. All challenges are to be accepted and played within two weeks, or else it's a forfeit. The tournament fee is $20.00, and each match costs the winner $2.00. The loser pays the time bill. The ladder club has officers and a committee to settle differences. There's prize money, too.

If you wish to know more about this format, write to Chicagoan **Frank Bondzinski**, a veteran three-cushion player. His address is 1301 Ironwood Drive, Mount Prospect, Ill. 60056-1441.

Open Letter To The Billiard Player

Please consider this a plea towards billiard players to cough up some money...not now of course, but when you pass away. You are going to leave this world and will leave large sums of money to your heirs. After some years, it is possible that your donation will not be remembered, and this would be unfortunate.

Your great-grand children may not know that you ever existed, and most likely will insist they worked hard for their money. It is likely that within fifty years your name will not be a household word...it's sad, but probable. Unless you are determined, you will leave your assets to these relatives anyway and when you do, you may think that all's well, but there will be some unhappy people who received too little, and they will surely dislike you.

I have a plan, however to have your name in lights for many years (much like King Tut,) and still satisfy your relatives. First of all, your kin do not know how much money will be available. Secondly, if you take twenty percent of your estate and set it aside for a great cause, they will probably never miss it. They will be proud that you supported a cause that was dear to your heart...one of the most compelling involvements that mankind has invented, and the one you enjoyed for so many years, the three-cushion billiard game.

Here's how it works: upon your demise, leave twenty percent of your assets in the hands of a Swiss banker, with carefully-written directions of how your money is to be invested, and how the yearly interest is to go into *your tournament fund*. Take inflation into account. Those of you that can leave $100,000 can probably put $8000 a year (8% net interest) into the coffers.

Establish this tournament every five years in your name, so your total contribution will be about $50,000. This, along with entry fees, can establish a $75,000 tournament...largest ever in the USA.

More Letter

The national billiard fathers can oversee the contests, and if enough persons answer this call, all kinds of things can happen. You could establish a tournament that's named after you, such as the; **Carl Liebovich's** Open...**Dan Segal's** Grand Prix...**Chris Crisman's** Grand Slam...**Sid Banner's** Two-Man Team Open...**Ray Mortell's** Woman's Open...**John Ringling North's** National Handicap...**Rich Schraeger's** Chicago Open...**Gerry Kolb's** 3-Cushion Meet...**Vic Kastil's** Pro-Pool Player Open...**Leonard Redlich's** Pro-Am...**Don Sperber's** 3-Cushion Classic...**Jerry Karsh's** National Four-Man Team Title...**Hernando Pinera's**...Miami-Pan-American.

You will draw many USA pool players that can handle a cue, since we have a zillion great pool players that earn very little. Having this caliber of cuemanship compete in three-cushion tournaments is mind-boggling. Don't forget we have some up and coming good three-cushion billiard players on the scene. If only both could compete for some worthwhile money...generosity could make that difference.

Several persons contributing could make a huge difference, such as the person that could leave $300,000, or one million. This infusion of money could move our country's billiard game into high gear. A $30,000 gift would provide a sizeable prize every five years. Best of all, a new level of USA billiard activity will be established for many future years providing a nice base to build on. This entire appeal can apply anywhere in the world such as the USA, Greece, Turkey, Korea, Argentina, Mexico...or anywhere 3-C billiards is loved. You are going to pass through this world only once. Let's see how long you can get your name to be a household word, and elevate this wonderful billiard game at the same time. Just phone your attorney and sign your name. Please be reminded that this is probably the area closest to your heart, and the one with the most beauty, and one that could use some help.

Iron Willie

In the state of Michigan, and sometimes in Florida, there is a robot named "*Iron Willie*." He is used for finding many answers to old problems concerning the pool game. One of his experiments dealt with measuring cue-ball deflection/curve. The results have cue makers pumping out cue shafts with less deflection.

Some day, "Iron Willie" will experiment with conditions the carom billiard world faces, which is that of fast cloth, fast cushions, and big heavy carom balls, all with lots of slide. When this occurs, more answers will be available.

Speed photography, showing deflection/curve with various speeds, would help greatly, and the *distances* could be better defined.

Dennis Dieckman is an expert in this area. If you want a custom cue stick that takes this into account, see him. Along with being a noted cue maker, he also conducts a school that teaches the art of cue making, which is located at his laboratory.

Don't forget his famous video-tapes on cue-making. You can reach **Dennis** at 313-428-1161.

Misc

Due to upcoming Olympics, the cue games are on the brink of further expansion. Soon the cue games will be included, and this will increase their popularity. My guess is the European community will not allow the USA pool players to dominate the games, and three-cushion billiards will make it's way into Olympic competition.

Meanwhile getting our act together seems hopeless. Our great champion **Sang Lee**, however, is busy teaching some upcoming players how to improve, and some currently accompany him to international contests. Because of his efforts, we will field a competent USA team, in spite of our small billiard population.

The world's top ten players currently have averages between 1.34 and 1.59. Recent world cup rankings have the balance of the top 20 players, between .976 to1.34.

Other 1996 **team** tournament averages are; Spain 1.02, Portugal .910, Mexico 1.077, Columbia .954, Nicaragua .806, Costa Rica .794, Venezuela .605, Uruguay .696, Chile .651, Bolivia .534, Dutch Junior tournament average .742, Austria Seniors top average .511 and BWA World Cup in Austria .856.

Gerard Klinkert, a noted Dutch billiard teacher and coach, has two hundred students at all times, yet our best players may give only ten paid lessons a year...Have our students fallen into a deep sleep?

Thanks to **Gerard**, the Billiard Atlas II is translated into the Dutch language.

On the subject of safe play, **Semih Sayginer** states, " Why not, we do in Turkey."

Over a beer, a world cup player was overheard saying, " If **Raymond Ceulemans** did not play safe, he would still be world champion."

Via Robert Byrne

Book endings like to go out with a flourish, and offering this system fits nicely here. If there was only one system to teach a beginner, this is it. This remarkable method was first called to my attention during a billiard tournament in Miami, Florida. **Robert Byrne** asked me if I had ever heard of the O*pposite-Three System.* When he sketched it out, I realized that this was unknown to me. He further stated that it came out of the dark ages from a famous USA 3-cushion player.

In order to check it out, we drove to **Bill Maloney's** Corner Pocket in Fort Lauderdale, which incidentally, was a hair-raising expressway car ride. After a thorough examination, it appeared that **Byrne** had indeed revived a valuable billiard system. **Byrne**, the noted author, decided to print this in the next issue of the Billiards Digest, in March of 1996, thus offering it to the billiard world, and to the Billiard Atlas III.

This system proposes that a cue ball aimed at the rail edge at diamond 3 will have a mirror image hit point of the cue-ball origin point. Drawing 75 shows the cue ball aimed at diamond 3, and the cue ball origin is Point A. The fourth-rail hit point is Point B, which is the mirror image of Point A. Note that Points A & B have the same distance to their respective corners, thus being mirror images.

Drawing 76 shows the cue ball located badly, and your desire in this situation is to hit Point B. Find the mirror image of Point B (or Point A,) then sight a line from Point A, through the rail edge at diamond 3, then to a spot on the wall about seven feet past the table.

Aim your cue ball at the spot on the wall to hit Point B. Employ a level cue and two tips of high running cue-ball english. Use four-rail cue ball speed and a full follow-through stroke.

Drawing 75

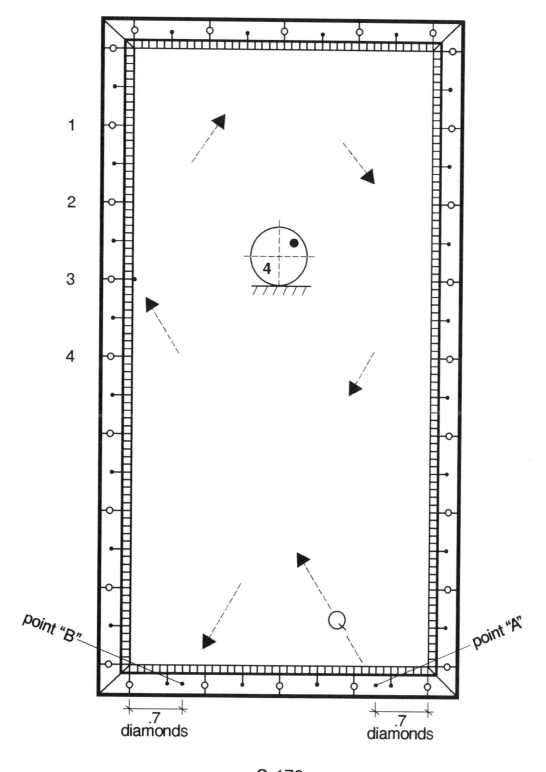

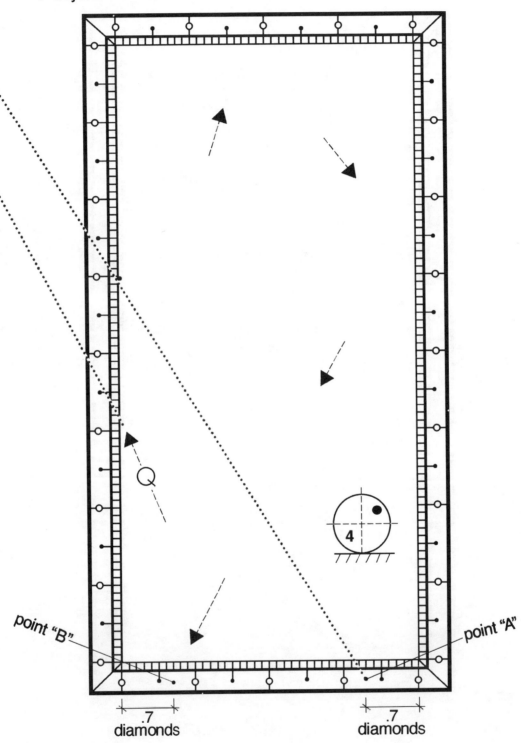

More Byrne

The *Opposite-Three System* can have cue ball origins from the long rail.

Drawing 77 indicates this by having Point A as the cue-ball origin. The mirror image of Point A is Point B, which is the desired fourth rail hit point. From Point A, aim at the rail edge at diamond 3, and the cue ball will arrive at Point B.

Drawing 78 shows the cue ball located badly, but the desired hit point is still Point B. Sight a line from Point A, through the rail edge at diamond 3, to a spot on the wall about six feet past the table. To arrive at Point B, aim your cue ball at the spot on the wall, and mark the first rail-hit point.

Try this system from a cue-ball origin point on the table (not a rail edge) such as point C. The mirror image point of Point C is Point D. Aim the cue ball at rail edge of diamond 3, and see if the cue ball arrives at point D. Use the spot on the wall principle when the cue ball is not located at Point C.

When caroming off an object ball to a spot on the wall, the cue ball english has to be adjusted, or slightly adjust the marked first-rail hit point. This adjustment varies because of a cue-ball curve.

This system works within certain boundaries, so use your stroke to find these limitations.

The distance to the spot on the wall beyond the table has to be fairly accurate. This is measured by using the same distance between the cue-ball origin point and the first-rail hit point. This distance can be between five and ten feet.

Drawing 77

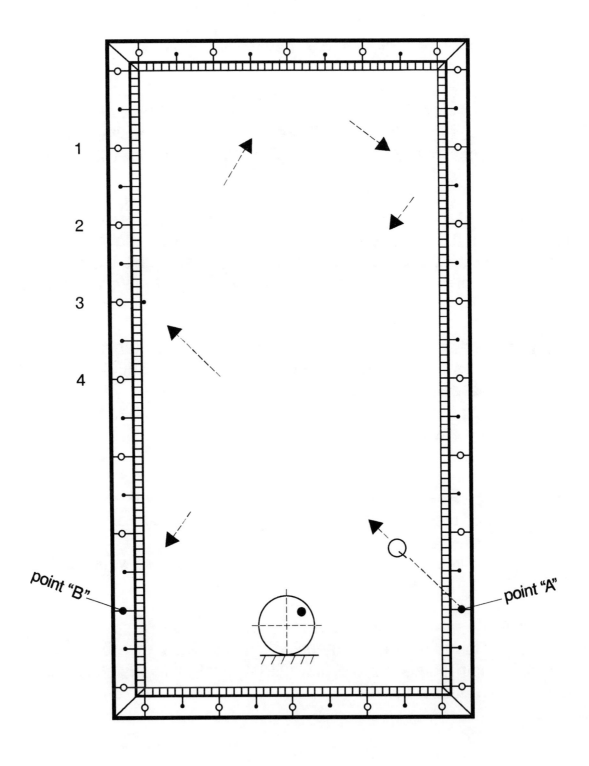

C-182

Drawing 78

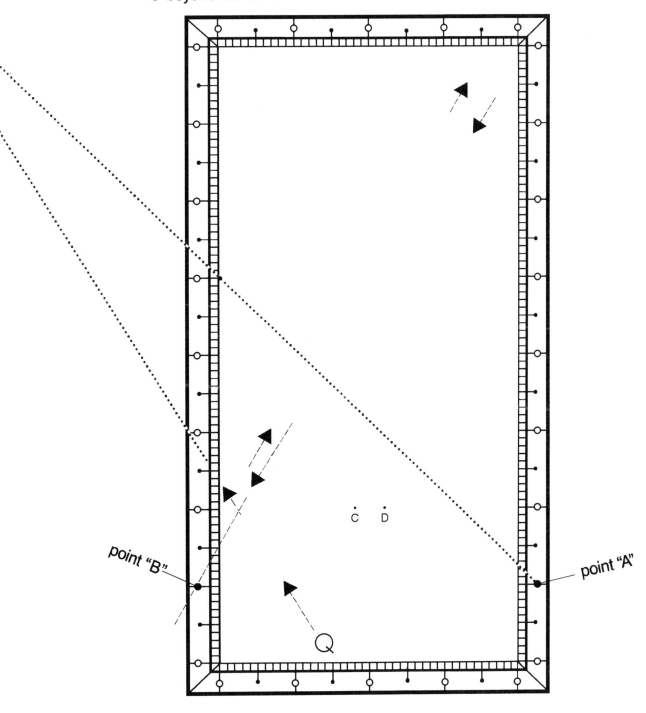

Authors Note

This Billiard Atlas III contains some terrific material. I only wish this information was available fifty years ago.

Usually techniques take a back seat to systems, but this book has some outstanding ones. The *Dive Back,* and *Frozen Object Ball-* techniques seem to come up constantly. Adding the *Spread 2.8* and *Spread 1.4* techniques to my repertoire, made certain difficult shots much easier.

Knowing how speed affects *cue side movement* was first-rate. This, with the *Magic Cure* and the *Mental Game,* made me realize what I had missed by not knowing the fundamentals.

How often have you heard a top player admit to using only **feel** ? My suspicion is that the very important area of *knowledge* was not discussed. After all, how do you use *feel* successfully when you lack *knowledge*? It is impossible to handle kisses and position if you don't know the running lines.

How about first learning the *fundamentals*, then study *systems and techniques* to learn how to make billiards? Calculating the running lines is key. While practicing systems, *employ feel.*

In the past, I have hedged on this subject and as of this writing my opinion is that *feel* is only as good as a players *knowledge.*

To illustrate this point, your attention is called to the *Opposite Three* system. Can you imagine how different a players game would be if this system was known when he first started playing? The same applies to the information in this book along with the past Atlas books, since it would have changed his progress dramatically.

Incidentally, it's never too late to start...

Glossary

Average: Number of points per inning, achieved by a player.

Cushion: The border surrounding the playing surface of the table, from which balls rebound, and also known as the rail.

English: The spin applied to a cue ball by striking it off center.

Draw: Spin applied by striking the cue ball below center.

Follow: Cue ball english that causes the cue ball to roll forward after contact with the object ball.

Kiss: An accidental contact between two balls that causes the shot to fail or score.

Masse: A shot in which the butt of the cue is raised at a high angle and strikes the cue ball from above.

Miss: Failure to score a billiard.

Position: A placement of the cue ball and object balls allowing the next shot to be uncomplicated.

Reverse English: Cue ball spin that is contrary to its natural motion after striking a cushion.

Reverse-the-rail: A shot in which a cue ball makes contact with a rail, then a second rail, then the first rail again, to score a three rail billiard.

Running English: Cue ball spin that favors a balls progress after it strikes a rail.

Safety: When a player misses scoring and leaves his opponent a difficult shot pattern.

Short Rail: An end rail, so called because it is half the length of a side, or long rail.

Shot: An attempt at scoring a billiard

Skid: Low cue ball spin which stops a rolling motion for a designed distance.

Slide: Where balls rebound at a wider angle due to new cloth or new balls.

Ticky: A shot that where the cue ball strikes the same rail twice, then a third rail or more, to score a billiard.

Track: A predictable cue ball path.

Umbrella: A shot where the cue ball strikes two or more cushions before hitting the first object ball.

The *Illustrated Encyclopedia of Billiards* has been the source of much of the above information. **Mike Shamos** is the author of this wonderful reference book. This is a must for your library.

Excerpts From Book Reviews and Players Comments

For years Harris has followed some of the world's best masters of the 3-cushion game, finding out the know how of billiard systems, techniques and tips from such players as Kobayashi, Komori, Sang Lee, Ashby, Bitalis, etc., etc....these were collected by Walter Harris, who considers himself a billiard reporter, and put into two books, volume I & II. These really unique study books named the "Billiard Atlas" will be arriving onto the Dutch market to help the 3-cushion player and eventually the Belgium player, and they can profit from the knowledge of these top players. A "must" for every 3-cushion player who wants to improve his game tremendously
GERARD KLINKERT book review in Holland's BILJART Magazine

I am amazed at the content; even in Japan we do not have this kind of book. So many systems that I have never dreamed of, attracts me. I cannot wait for the day when "book three" is put into publication
NAKATANI TOMOAKI, Japanese University Student

More Secrets are in the open. Carom players shouldn't miss this book. Can give you the edge for winning 9 ball, one pocket and even 8-ball.
TOM SHAW Book review in POOL AND BILLIARD Magazine

Books like yours are what give me the most enjoyment in billiards. Sure, it's nice to win games and all that, but what I really enjoy is learning how the game works.
RON SEITZ, West Point, New York

It is very refreshing to know that there are a few people left in this world that still care enough about the sport to pass on a little of what they know. Your book is not so far over my head as other books are.
DWIGHT BARRY, Sao Paulo, Brazil

Walt Harris, a builder tycoon on pension from Florida, travels the billiard circus and markets his accurate systems. The billiard church is divided on the question "What makes a top player, system or feeling, calculation or intuition?". The masters have memorized over a 100,000 games and pictures. With his systems Harris promises the beginner quick success. His books talk about angles, the mathematics of the diamond markings on the cushions, and their secrets. With his accurate playing diagrams, Harris has ended a dark era.
1995 "DER SPIEGAL" Magazine book review

The Atlas books show that the author cares for the game's promotion, something that seldom happens in the billiard world. Your diamond system is "impressive". In the past there was not much to use, maybe the old systems of Roger Condi or Willie Hoppe, or basic instinct. I will never know what the world class players use, as they keep them secrets.
MICHAEL CACOULIDIS, Thessaloniki, Greec

Credits.....volume III

Banner, Sid 175
Billiard Digest 178 thru 183
Bitalis, Richard 36, 147, 164
Blomdahl, Torbjorn 147
Bondzinski, Frank 173
Byrne, Robert 177 thru 183
Cho, Sonny 170
Chrisman, Chris 173, 175

Cochran, Welker 136
Cook, Stephen 2 thru 6
Ceulemans, Raymond 144, 147, 169, 170, 172, 177
Dieckman, Dennis 176
Gwinn, Joe 138, 139
Hallon, Carlos 167, 170
Hoppe, Willie 59, 136, 138
Jasper, Dick 141, 146
Karsh, Jerry 175
Kastil, Vic 175

Kilgore, Ray 177 thru 183
Klinkert, Gerard 177
Kobayshi, Nobuski 114, 115
Kolb, Gerry 175
Komori, Junichi 147
Liebovich, Carl 175
Martin, Johanna VII
Maloney, Bill 178
Mortell, Ray 175
Navarra, Enrique V
Mosconi, Willie Navarra, Enrique V
North, John 175
Pineras, Hernando 175
Pool and Billiard Magazine 138, 139
Redlich, Leonard 175
Reyes, Efren 147, 169
Robin, Eddie 146
Sang Lee 117, 122, 147, 158, 159 thru 165, 167, 169, 177
Sayginer, Semih 144, 177
Schraeger, Rich 175
Segal, Dan 130, 142, 143, 176

Shooni, Mazin 170
Sperber, Don 175
Tomoaki, Nakatani 60, 61, 120
World Report, 3-Cushion 138, 139

Index.....volume III

Across The Table   31, 57
Author's Note   179
Ball   166, 167
Ball   124, 127, 128
Ball Side Movement   112, 113
Bank Tickie   28, 29
Basic Diamond System   109, 110
Blue Moon   85 thru 95
Chapters   1, 31, 59, 71, 97, 117,
Coaching   171
Cue Align   111
Cushions   158 thru 165
Dive Back   36, 37, 135, 149, 157, 169
Easy Across   32 thru 35
End Rail   71 thru 95
Equal Angle   54, 55
Equipment   157 thru 167
Fifty Innings   173
Florida Back Up   20 thru 24
Formats   172, 173
Forward   XI
Frozen Object Ball   64 thru 69
Frozen Short   122, 123
Fundamentals   135 thru 147
Great Advice   7, 11, 19, 25, 41, 63, 79
Introduction   VIII, IX
Iron Willie   176
Joey's   124, 126, 130, 132
Kirikaeshi   60, 61, 62, 118, 120
Long Angle   1 thru 29, 158, 160
Lucky Five   12 thru 18, 118, 121
Lucky Seven   124, 129, 85, 133, 137, 155, 161
Magic Cure   138, 139
Max Across   46 thru 49
Mental Game   149 thru 154
Mirror Mirror   104, 105
Misc   169 thru 177
Miss-A-kiss-A-Day   98, 99
Open Letter   174, 175
Opposite Three   178 thru 183
Parallel Across   52, 53
Paralleling   102, 103
Position   146
Rhythm   140, 141
Rising Sun   124, 125
Sid's Cousin   26, 27
Spot On The Wall   106, 108
Spread 2.8   38, 39, 40
Spread 1.4   42 thru 45
Stroke   138, 139
Stroke Styles   147
Survey   170
Theory   144, 145
Tokyo Connection   72 thru 87
Triangulate   50, 51
Wow   56, 57, 100, 101
Wrist   142, 143

Pam Stone of Cocoa Beach, FL. helped with the editing

Our printer is Mark Lawrence of Sharp Offset Printing, Rutland, VT

Notes

Notes

Notes